Intercultural Awareness

CLIL

Content & Language Integrated Learning

Shigeru Sasajima

Taizo Kudo

Hongtao Jing

Larry Joe

Hannah Haruna

SANSHUSHA

音声ダウンロード＆ストリーミングサービス（無料）のご案内

https://www.sanshusha.co.jp/onsei/isbn/9784384334944/

本書の音声データは、上記アドレスよりダウンロードおよびストリーミング再生ができます（付属CDと内容は同じです）。ぜひご利用ください。

はじめに

　本書は、CLIL (Content and Language Integrated Learning)（内容と言語を統合した学習）という教育理念を基盤として構成してあります。内容（題材）として intercultural awareness（文化間意識）を扱い、高校や大学などで学ぶ身近な話題をグローバルな視点から英語コミュニケーション能力を育成できるように工夫しました。扱う題材も著者の背景もさまざまです。英語に焦点を当てていますが、多言語多文化状況がますます進展する社会でどのように交流し、共生し、学習し、仕事をしたらよいのかを、学習者が考えることを期待しています。

　CLIL は、内容 (Content)、思考 (Cognition)、コミュニケーション (Communication)、文化間理解 (Culture) という、「4つの C」(4Cs) を考慮して学ぶことを大切にしています。本書はそのなかの Culture に焦点を当てています。特に Intercultural Communicative Competence (ICC)（文化間コミュニケーション能力）の育成を大きな目標としています。

　コンピュータやメディアの発達によりコミュニケーションが容易になりましたが、そのために逆に人間関係がよりむずかしい世界になっている可能性があります。ある一つの価値観や態度や作法や知識では対応がうまくいかず、英語が多少できたとしても文化的につまずき、問題が起こる場合もあります。また、英語だけでは限界があります。日本もますます複言語複文化の意識（plurilingual and pluricultural awareness）（いくつかの言語を生涯通じて学び、多様な文化に対応できる意識）が必要になることは間違いありません。本書の目的はその基礎的な力を育成することです。

　学習者の英語力は、CEFR の 6 レベルの B1（一部 B2）を想定していますが、リスニングとスピーキングについては、A2 程度で十分学習可能な内容です。学習者によっては多少むずかしい部分もありますが、英語の難易度に縛られることなく、内容にこだわり、設定されている Task に取り組み、教科書の話題から多様な話題に興味を広げて自律的に学んでください。学習を通じて、「グローバル市民 (Global citizen)」として将来活躍する人材が出てきてくれたら嬉しい限りです。

　なお、本書では、一般的に使われている「異文化」という表現を使わず、「文化間」という用語を使っています。理由は、英語の「inter-」には「異」という意味がないからです。「intercultural awareness」は「互いの文化を意識して理解する」という意味で、その点を重視します。

著者一同

Contents

Unit 1

Develop Your Intercultural Awareness …………………… 13
文化間意識を高める

Chinese students' intercultural citizenship　中国の学生の文化間の市民意識

New employees' global awareness　新入社員のグローバル意識

Unit 2

Understand Intercultural Diversity in Peoples and Places ………… 19
人と場所の文化間多様性を理解する

Refugee admission or recognition　難民受入と認定

Muslims in the US　アメリカ合衆国のイスラム

Unit 3

Be a Good Consumer …………………………………………… 25
買い物上手になる

Mass production　大量生産

Tradition vs Industrialization　伝統工芸品と工業化

Unit 4

Learn about Food, Culture and Society ………………… 31
食物、文化、社会について知る

Vegan　ベジタリアン

Obesity　肥満

Unit 5

Have Better Lifestyles in Different Cultures ………… 37
文化に応じたより良い生活スタイルを送る

Paternity leave　男性育児休暇

Homework　宿題

Unit 6

Be an Intercultural Traveler ………………………………… 43
互いの文化を理解する旅行者となる

Inbound and outbound tourists in Japan　訪日（外国人）旅行者と海外（日本人）旅行者

Countries that attract tourists　ツーリストを魅了する国

Unit 7

Cultivate Global Citizenship ………………………………… 49
地球市民感覚を培う

Students' views of global citizen　大学生にとって地球市民とは？

Global citizenship poll　地球市民意識調査

本教科書の構成と学習展開

　本教科書は、15 ユニットから構成され、文化間意識、経済、社会、健康、旅行、教育、芸術、コンピュータ、ジェンダー、戦争、グローバル化など、多様な課題を扱っています。他の科目の学習内容と関連させながら学習活動を展開すると効果的なので、必ずしも Unit 1 から学習する必要はありません。また、すべてのユニットを学ぶ必要もありません。興味関心に沿って柔軟に対応してください。

　英語力の到達目標は、読む、聞くにおいて CEFR の B1 ～ B2、話す（会話と発表）、書くにおいては A2 ～ B1 程度を想定していますが、授業内での活動や家庭学習のなかで自律的な学習を発展的に行うことを期待しています。また、文化間意識を培うことも大きな目標にしています。CAN DO で示した自己評価表を活用して、グローバルに活躍できる基礎的な力を身につけてほしいと考えています。

　各ユニットは次のように構成されています。

1　Brainstorming　話題に興味関心を抱く
Warm up と Task (listening, shadowing, talk) を通じて活動しながら考える

2　Word info 1　話題に関連する語句と内容の理解を深める
Task を通じて語句に習熟し、話し合う

3　Word info 2　話題に関連する語句と内容の理解を深める
Task を通じて知識や文化について考える

4　Reading graphs & charts 1　グラフや図などを読み取り、関心を広げる
Task を通じて知識を深め、さらに調べ互いに理解を深める

5　Reading graphs & charts 2　グラフや図などを読み取り、関心を広げる
Task を通じて知識を深め、さらに調べ互いに理解を深める

6　Discussion & presentation　話題に関する会話を聞き、話す
会話内容を確認して、Task に沿って話し合うか、発表してみる

CLIL の学習

英語学習は、単語をおぼえる、文法ルールを理解する、英文を読んで訳す、音読する、会話のパターンをおぼえて練習する、英語を聞き取って質問に答える、などの学習活動が多く、「テストのための勉強」という傾向にあります。基礎学習はもちろん重要です。CLIL でもその点は重視します。文化という観点でも、国際理解が中心的な学習対象となり、それぞれの国と地域の社会文化習慣などの知識の理解に重点が置かれることが多いのが現状です。本教科書は、CLIL 教育の観点から、そのような伝統的な知識や技能を重視したアプローチよりは、英語で伝える内容や意味のやりとりに重点を置き、授業中の友達との会話、考え方の違いなどを、英語と日本語で互いに考えることを重視しています。

CLIL は基本的にバイリンガル (bilingual) ですが、従来よりは柔軟に考えて、英語と日本語が交差するようなイメージで使用される状況を重視します。これを translanguaging と英語で言います。trans- は「超えて、渡って、変換して、交差して」などの意味を持ち、languaging は「言語する」という動詞の扱いです。日本語で言うと、「言語を交差させて使う」というような意味になります。多言語状況の地域ではごくふつうの状況です。これを CLIL は積極的に考えています。

英語だけでやりとりすることは多くの学習者にとってはむずかしいことです。しかし、英語学習において英語を使うことは基本的に大切なことです。部分的にでもできる限り英語でやりとりする、あるいは書くという活動は欠かせません。正確に英語を使うことは大切ですが、ふつうのコミュニケーションでは「間違い」は頻繁にあります。それよりも伝える「内容」の方がもっと大切です。

CLIL では「為すことによって学ぶ (learning by doing)」ということを基本にしています。それは意味をともなうことです。コミュニケーションをうまくするためには、伝えたい意味があり内容があり、そのために考えなければいけない文化間理解が必要なのです。次の学びの基本を意識して学習してください。

CLIL の学びの基本

- ・目標を明確にして、学ぶ内容に興味を持ち、評価する
- ・日本語に訳すことにこだわらず、意味を理解し、英語を自然に使う
- ・自分の持っている知識を使って推測する
- ・英語の誤りを気にしないで、英語で意味を伝える
- ・互いに協力して教え合い、学び合う
- ・興味のあることは自分で調べ、わからないことは遠慮しないで質問する
- ・英語と日本語の両方を使い、意味のやりとりを意識する

文化間意識を培う CAN DO

　本教科書は、ICC（Intercultural Communicative Competence: 文化間コミュニケーション能力）の育成を、CLIL 学習を通じて目指しています。その達成度を自己評価するために、ヨーロッパ評議会 (Council of Europe) が Reference Framework of Competences for Democratic Culture (2018) を提示しています。そこに掲載されている 135 項目の文化間意識の到達度を確認するディスクリプター (key descriptor) の基礎項目を参考に、日本の状況に合わせた 44 項目の CAN DO 自己評価表を作成しました。下記の「民主的文化のための能力モデル (Model of Competencies for Democratic Culture)」の図を根拠にしてあります。

Model of Competences for Democratic Culture
（民主的文化のための能力モデル）

Values
- Valuing human dignity and human rights
  （人間の尊厳と権利を認める）
- Valuing cultural diversity（文化の多様性を認める）
- Valuing democracy, justice, fairness, equality and the rule of law
  （デモクラシー、正当、公平、平等、法を認める）

Attitudes
- Openness to cultural otherness and to other beliefs, world views and practices
  （文化的な他者や他の信条、世界観、実践の受容）
- Respect（尊敬）・Civic-mindedness（市民感覚）
- Responsibility（責任）・Self-efficacy（自己効力感）
- Tolerance of ambiguity（曖昧さの寛容）

Competence

Skills
- Autonomous learning skills（自律学習）
- Analytical and critical thinking skills（分析的批判的思考）
- Skills of listening and observing（聞き観察）
- Empathy（共感）
- Flexibility and adaptability（柔軟と適応）
- Linguistic, communicative and plurilingual skills
  （言語、コミュニケーション、複言語）
- Co-operation skills（協力）
- Conflict-resolution skills（問題解決）

Knowledge and critical understanding
- Knowledge and critical understanding of the self
  （自己の知識と批判的理解）
- Knowledge and critical understanding of language and communication（言語とコミュニケーションの知識と批判的理解）
- Knowledge and critical understanding of the world: politics, law, human rights, culture, cultures, religions, history, media, economies, environment, sustainability
  （政治、法、人権、文化、宗教、歴史、メディア、経済、環境、持続性などの世界の知識と批判的理解）

　Competence、つまり ICC は、Values（価値を認める）、Attitudes（態度）、Skills（技能）、Knowledge and critical understanding（知識と批判的理解）から構成されると考えています。詳細は上記の図のとおりです。それにもとづいて、次のように 44 項目の CAN DO ディスクリプターで、学習者自身が 4 段階で判断してください。自己評価では、コースを開始する際に該当する段階に○をつけてください。その後コースの進度に沿って適宜参照してください。最後にコースの終わりの段階でふりかえりのなかで該当する項目に◎をつけて比較してください。

　　　　1　コースの開始　○　　　　　　2　コースの終了　◎

重要なことは、自分を見つめることで、成績のために自己評価をすることではありません。自己評価をする際は、話し合いながらすることが重要です。言葉だけの評価ではなく、具体的な行動の評価です。自己評価しながら、ICC を培うことが大切です。

	CAN DO Self-assessment for Intercultural Awareness （文化間意識のための CAN DO 自己評価表）	Disagree (否)			Agree (諾)
1	I can say that human rights should always be protected and respected. 人権はいつも守られ尊重されるべきと言うことができる。	1	2	3	4
2	I can say that specific rights of children should be respected and protected by society. 子供の権利は社会において尊重され守られるべきと言うことができる。	1	2	3	4
3	I can promote the view that we should be tolerant of the different beliefs that are held by others in society. 社会の中で他の人が抱く異なる信条を受け入れるべきという考えを促すことができる。	1	2	3	4
4	I can promote the view that one should always strive for mutual understanding and meaningful dialogue between people and groups who are perceived to be "different" from one another. 互いに「違う」と考える人やグループ間の相互理解や意味ある会話を、いつも人は模索すべきという考えを推し進めることができる。	1	2	3	4
5	I can say that schools should teach students about democracy and how to act as a democratic citizen. 学校は民主主義やその市民としてどう行動するかについて生徒に指導すべきと言うことができる。	1	2	3	4
6	I can express the view that all citizens should be treated equally and impartially under the law. すべての市民は法の下に等しく隔たりなく扱われるべきという観点を表明することができる。	1	2	3	4
7	I can say that laws should always be fairly applied and enforced. 法は常に公平に適応され執行されるべきと言うことができる。	1	2	3	4
8	I can show interest in learning about people's beliefs, values, traditions and world views. 人々の信条、価値観、伝統、世界観について学ぶことに興味を示すことができる。	1	2	3	4
9	I can express interest in travelling to other countries. 他の国に旅行に行くことに興味を示すことができる。	1	2	3	4
10	I can give space to others to express themselves. 他の人に意見を述べる間を与えることができる。	1	2	3	4
11	I can express respect for others as equal human beings. 他の人に人間として等しく敬意を表明することができる。	1	2	3	4
12	I can express a willingness to co-operate and work with others. 他の人と協力し作業する喜びを表明することができる。	1	2	3	4
13	I can collaborate with others for common interest causes. 他の人と共通の興味を起因として協力することができる。	1	2	3	4

CAN DO Self-assessment for Intercultural Awareness (文化間意識のための CAN DO 自己評価表)	Disagree (否)			Agree (諾)
14 I can accept responsibility for my actions. 自分の行動の責任を取ることができる。	1	2	3	4
15 I can apologize if I hurt someone's feelings. 誰かの感情を損ねたら謝罪することができる。	1	2	3	4
16 I can express a belief in my own ability to understand issues. 物事を理解する自身の能力を信じることを表明することができる。	1	2	3	4
17 I can carry out activities that I have planned. 計画したことを実行することができる。	1	2	3	4
18 I can engage well with others who have a variety of different points of view.　異なる考え方を持つ他の人とうまくやっていくことができる。	1	2	3	4
19 I can suspend judgments about others temporarily. 他の人についての判断を一時的に保留することができる。	1	2	3	4
20 I can show ability to identify resources for learning (e.g. people, books, internet). 学習リソース（人、本、インターネットなど）を見つける能力を示すことができる。	1	2	3	4
21 I can seek clarification of new information from others when needed.　他の人からの新しい情報を必要なときに確認を求めることができる。	1	2	3	4
22 I can identify similarities and differences between new information and what is already known. 新しい情報とすでに知っていることの類似と相違を認めることができる。	1	2	3	4
23 I can use evidence to support my opinions. 自分の意見を支持する証拠を示すことができる。	1	2	3	4
24 I can listen carefully to differing opinions. 異なる意見を注意して聞くことができる。	1	2	3	4
25 I can listen attentively to others. 他の人の言うことをきちんと聞くことができる。	1	2	3	4
26 I can recognize when a companion needs my help. 仲間が自分の助けを必要とするときを認識できる。	1	2	3	4
27 I can express sympathy for the bad things that I have seen happen to other people. 他の人に起こると思う悪いことに対して共感を示すことができる。	1	2	3	4
28 I can modify my opinions if I am shown through rational argument that this is required. 決定した結果がこちらが必要だということを示せば、自分の意見を修正できる。	1	2	3	4
29 I can change the decisions that I have made if the consequences of those decisions show that this is required. こちらが必要だという結果が示されれば、決定したことを変更することができる。	1	2	3	4
30 I can express my thoughts on a problem. 問題に関して自分の考えを表明することができる。	1	2	3	4

CAN DO Self-assessment for Intercultural Awareness （文化間意識のための CAN DO 自己評価表）	Disagree (否)			Agree (諾)

31 I can ask speakers to repeat what they have said if it wasn't clear to me.　あまり明確でない場合は話し手が言ったことをくり返すように言うことができる。

1	2	3	4

32 I can build positive relationships with others in a group.
グループの他の人と積極的な関係を築くことができる。

1	2	3	4

33 I can do my share of the group's work when working as a member of a group.
あるグループのメンバーとして活動するときは自分の役割をすることができる。

1	2	3	4

34 I can communicate with conflicting parties in a respectful manner.
対立する団体と敬意をもってコミュニケーションできる。

1	2	3	4

35 I can identify options for resolving conflicts.
対立を解決するために意見を認めることができる。

1	2	3	4

36 I can describe my own motivations.
自分自身の動機づけを説明できる。

1	2	3	4

37 I can describe the ways in which my thoughts and emotions influence my behavior.
自分の考えや感情が自分の行動にどのように影響を与えるかを説明できる。

1	2	3	4

38 I can explain how tone of voice, eye contact and body language can aid communication.
声のトーン、アイコンタクト、ボディランゲージがコミュニケーションをどう助けるかを説明できる。

1	2	3	4

39 I can explain the meaning of basic political concepts, including democracy, freedom, citizenship, rights and responsibilities.
民主主義、自由、市民権、権利、義務など、政治の基本的なことの意味を説明できる。

1	2	3	4

40 I can explain why everybody has a responsibility to respect the human rights of others.
なぜ他の人の人権を尊重する責任が誰にもあるかを説明できる。

1	2	3	4

41 I can describe basic cultural practices (e.g. eating habits, greeting practices, ways of addressing people, politeness) in one other culture.
基本的な文化習慣（食事、挨拶、人の呼称、丁寧さなど）を互いの文化で説明できる。

1	2	3	4

42 I can reflect critically on how my own world view is just one of many world views.
いかに自分の世界観が多くの世界観の一つにすぎないかを批判的にふりかえることができる。

1	2	3	4

43 I can assess society's impact on the natural world, for example, in terms of population growth, population development, resource consumption.
人口増加、人口開発、資源消費など、自然界への社会の刺激を評価できる。

1	2	3	4

44 I can reflect critically on the risks associated with environmental damage.
環境破壊と関連するリスクについて批判的にふりかえることができる。

1	2	3	4

＊本自己評価表は Reference Framework of Competences for Democratic Culture (Council of Europe. 2018) を参照して作成。

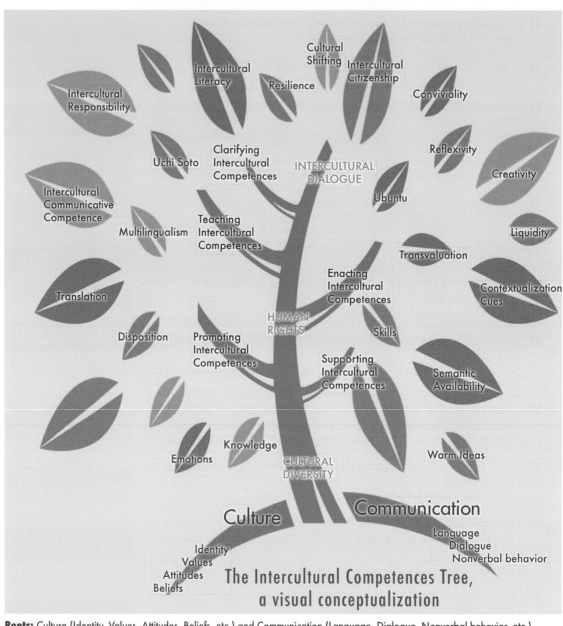

The Intercultural Competences Tree,
a visual conceptualization

Roots: Culture (Identity, Values, Attitudes, Beliefs, etc.) and Communication (Language, Dialogue, Nonverbal behavior, etc.)

Trunk: Cultural Diversity, Human Rights, Intercultural Dialogue

Branches: Operational steps (Clarifying, Teaching, Promoting, Supporting and Enacting Intercultural Competences)

Leaves: Intercultural Responsibility, Intercultural Literacy, Resilience, Cultural Shifting, Intercultural Citizenship, Conviviality, Reflexivity, Creativity, Liquidity, Contextualization Cues, Transvaluation, Ubuntu, Semantic Availability, Warm Ideas, Skills, Uchi Soto, Multilingualism, Disposition, Emotions, Knowledge, Translation, Intercultural Communicative Competence. Some of the leaves have been left free so that this Tree which is very much alive, can be complemented upon the rich diversity of contexts available worldwide.

(Source: UNESCO)

Develop Your Intercultural Awareness

文化間意識を高める

1 Brainstorming

Look at this figure. Do you know the name of the tree? It is called the "**Intercultural Competences Tree**" suggested by UNESCO. What do you see in the roots, trunk, branches and leaves?

UNESCO = The United Nations Educational, Scientific and Cultural Organization

• Warm up   Talk to your classmate(s), and then listen to the synopsis.

Task 1 Listen to the explanation and fill in the blanks.

01-01
001

In 2013, 1)_____ proposed the Intercultural Competences Tree as shown on the left. It is a symbolic 2)_____ of intercultural competences. The tree shows a number of the concepts of intercultural competences. First, look at the roots of the tree. You see two concepts: 3)_____ and 4)_____. Then you can find several sub-concepts under each concept: Identity, Values, Attitudes, Beliefs, Language, Dialogue, and Nonverbal behavior. Next, look at the trunk of the tree, and you can find three concepts: Cultural 5)_____, Human rights and Intercultural 6)_____. Finally, look at its branches and leaves. You see lots of concepts, such as Clarifying, 7)_____, Promoting, and Supporting. This tree displays how you can develop your intercultural competences. Let's develop your intercultural awareness through using this textbook.

Task 2 Do shadowing

01-02
002

Task 3 Talk in pairs

1) Do you think you have good intercultural awareness?
2) Look at the Intercultural Competences Tree. Which concept are you interested in?

Task 4 What is intercultural competence? Fill in the blanks with the appropriate words.

> globalization   skills   goals   learning

Intercultural competence is one of the specific 1)_____ in your lifelong 2)_____ today. It will also help you deal with the current state of diversity and 3)_____. Some researchers think that intercultural competence can be made of several elements: e.g. knowledge, 4)_____, and attitudes.

Task 5 Fill in the blank with the word that fits the definition.

> stereotype   multiculturalism   culture shock   low-context   high-context

1) (   ) is the discomfort which you experience when coming across and trying to adjust to unfamiliar cultural practices.
2) (   ) culture relies heavily on the context of an interaction to convey the message. Japanese people generally value this culture.
3) (   ) communication is explicit, so your words directly tell all the information, and there is always explicit meaning apart from the words. Scandinavian people generally value this culture.
4) (   ) is a widely held but fixed image or idea of a particular type of person or thing.
5) (   ) is a situation where different cultural or racial groups in a society have equal rights and opportunities and nobody is regarded as unimportant.

©hh 5800/iStockphoto.com

Task 6 Discuss in pairs

1) Do you know anyone that has intercultural competences?
2) Are you interested in cultures in other countries?
3) Have you communicated with people from other countries? If so, please share your experiences with your friends.

3 Word info 2

Task 7 Quiz

Q1 What does communicative competence mean to you? Why do you think so?

   a) skills of listening, speaking, reading and writing
   b) a learner's ability to use language to communicate successfully
   c) knowledge of a language including grammar and vocabulary

Q2 What does intercultural communicative competence mean to you? Why do you think so?

   a) the ability to communicate effectively in cross-cultural situations
   b) intercultural attitudes, knowledge, skills of interpreting and relating, skills of discovery and interaction, and critical cultural awareness
   c) understanding of cultural differences; experiencing other cultures; and self-awareness of one's own culture

Q3 What does intercultural citizen mean to you? Why do you think so?

   a) a second language speaker who can establish positive intercultural relationships in any interactions
   b) an individual with the development of intercultural communicative competence to engage in political activity
   c) an individual with a global or international identity
   d) an individual who identifies with being part of a global community

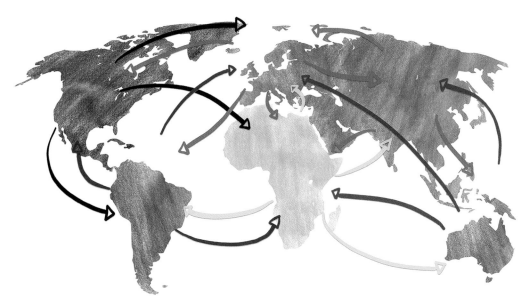

©Eike Leppert/iStockphoto

4 Reading graphs & charts 1

Chinese students' intercultural citizenship 中国の学生の文化間の市民意識

CD1-03
⬇ 003

Task 8 ▶ Fill in the blanks

Forms	Frequency	Percentage (%)
Lectures and courses delivered by foreign teachers	233	76
Public media (TV, Internet, newspaper, films, etc.)	216	70
Short-term visits abroad (studying, traveling, visiting relatives and friends overseas)	118	38
Making foreign friends	100	32
International communication experience	91	30
None	58	18

N=308.   (Source: Byram et al., 2016)

Research conducted by Michael Byram in 2016 explored how 1)_____ Chinese students thought about intercultural citizenship in English language learning. They were asked about what 2)_____ of activities they regarded as intercultural contact. The above table summarizes the responses from them. When you look at the 3)_____ , you can see the two major forms for students to have contact with other cultures. They are attending 4)_____ or courses delivered by 5)_____ teachers (233/76 %) and using the public 6)_____ such as the Internet, TV, and films (216/70 %). The other forms are short term 7)_____ abroad (118/38 %) and making foreign friends (100/32 %) and international 8)_____ experience (91/30 %).

Task 9 ▶ Do research and discuss

1) What kind of intercultural experiences do you have?
2) What intercultural activities should your school improve?
3) Ask your classmates about their intercultural experiences.

©Yue_/iStockphoto.com

5 | Reading graphs & charts 2

New employees' global awareness 新入社員のグローバル意識

Task 10 Fill in the blanks

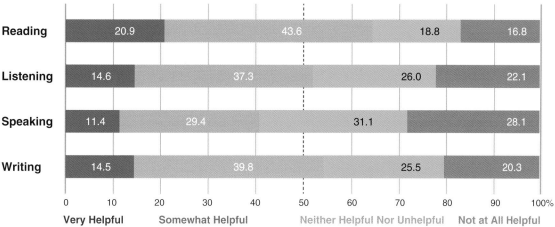

	Very Helpful	Somewhat Helpful	Neither Helpful Nor Unhelpful	Not at All Helpful
Reading	20.9	43.6	18.8	16.8
Listening	14.6	37.3	26.0	22.1
Speaking	11.4	29.4	31.1	28.1
Writing	14.5	39.8	25.5	20.3

Sangyo Noritsu University in Japan conducted a survey on the new employees' global awareness in 2017. According to the 1)_____, 60 % of them didn't want to work overseas, and 44.4 % of them answered that they were not confident in communicating in English well. Among the questions in the survey, one 2)_____ asked about the English education that they had had in their schools and universities. Look at the 3)_____ above. It shows how helpful they thought the education was for them to improve their 4)_____ of reading, listening, 5)_____ and writing. The table shows that the education they received was very or somewhat helpful for 6)_____ and 7)_____ for them, but it was not so helpful for listening. It is interesting that 59.2 % (31.1 % + 28.1 %) of the new employees thought the education they had was not helpful for 8)_____. This result suggests that they are not satisfied with their English 9)_____ ability.

Task 11 Do research and discuss

1) Why do you think many new employees are not confident in speaking English?
2) Do you think you can use English well? Which skill(s) are you good at?
3) What do you think about English education in Japan?

©itakayuki/iStockphoto.com

6 Discussion & presentation

CD1-05
↓ 005

Sakura and Xiaoxue are talking about intercultural citizens. What do you think about the underlined parts especially? Do you agree with their opinions?

S: I think today's class is very interesting! It is new for me to learn about intercultural citizens!

X: Yeah, this is also a new topic for me.

S: What do you think about intercultural citizens?

X: 1) I think intercultural citizens can share two or more languages and cultures together. They can learn a lot from each other and integrate cultures with other people without prejudice. How about you?

S: For me, 2) intercultural citizens have open-minds, are willing to try new things, and respect other people.

X: Yeah, I agree with you. The most important thing is that you must respect cultural differences. You shouldn't have any bias and think by yourself.

S: When I went to Yulin City, China, my friend ordered a plate of dog meat, but I didn't eat it. I think people should not eat dog, because dogs are our best and loyal friends or pets. I asked him, 'How could you eat dog meat?' He said this kind of dog is not a pet and dog meat is a traditional Chinese cuisine.

X: That must have been a big culture shock for you. The Yulin dog meat festival is a day that many local people celebrate by eating dog meat, which is their traditional custom.

S: I never eat dog meat, but I still respect the culture in Yulin.

X: Animal rights activists protest against the festival every year. 3) The government should make laws to protect dogs. I hope the festival will be closed quickly.

写真：AP / アフロ

> **Task 12** What do you think about Yulin dog meat festival? Have you experienced any culture shock? What do you think about intercultural citizens?

Understand Intercultural Diversity in Peoples and Places

人と場所の文化間多様性を理解しよう

1 Brainstorming

Look at this picture. It is a beautiful place, isn't it? This picture is fascinating. It has two things that don't often coexist easily: a church and a mosque. In history Muslims and Christians have sometimes had difficulty understanding each other. How do they live together in this area? Do they live peaceful lives or not?

©Sliderzero | Dreamstime.com

•Warm up Talk to your classmate(s), and then listen to the explanation.

01-06
006

Task 1 Listen to the explanation and fill in the blanks

Kazan is the capital city of the Republic of Tatarstan, Russia, with a population of over one

1)_____ . It has two main fascinating features. First, the city is famous for 2)_____

events. In 2009, Kazan was chosen as "the sport capital of Russia." Since then, many sports

events have been held in this area. The 3)_____ FIFA World Cup was one of them. Also,

the city is famous for its religious 4)_____ . Many Christians and Muslims live together in

this area. There are also churches and 5)_____ standing side by side. How did this kind of

coexistence emerge in Kazan? About five hundred years ago the people there couldn't accept

each other's 6)_____ . They had many battles over the centuries. However, thanks to

the historical 7)_____ who protested that mutual understanding is important for both

8)_____ , and because of the governmental shift from restrictions to 9)_____ of

religions in the country, people in 10)_____ have been enjoying religious coexistence

for decades.

Task 2 Do shadowing

1-07
007

Task 3 Talk in pairs

1) Do you want to go to Kazan?

2) Have you ever been to a church or a mosque?

3) What do you think about different religions?

2 Word info 1

Task 4 ▸ Quiz

Q1 What does it mean? Which photo does it show?

a) mosque   • a building used for Christian religious activities

b) shrine   • a building in which Jews meet for religious worship

c) temple   • a place dedicated to the worship of gods or deities

d) church   • a Muslim place of public worship

e) synagogue   • a place of worship and the dwellings of the gods or deities

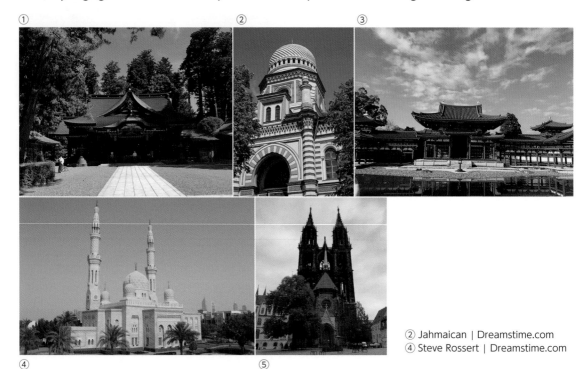

② Jahmaican | Dreamstime.com
④ Steve Rossert | Dreamstime.com

Q2 Which of the following best describes taboos?

a) asking Muslims what kind of food they can't eat

b) talking with Christians about alcohol

c) passing food from chopstics to chopsticks

d) entering into a house without removing your shoes

Task 5 ▸ Discuss in pairs

Have you ever broken any taboos unconsciously? If so, talk about the experience with your partner. If not, think about how we can avoid such a situation.

3 Word info 2

Task 6 Fill in the blanks with appropriate words. Which topic is interesting to you? Why do you think so?

> Christians   African Americans   Maori   coexistence   discrimination   exclusion

1) 1)_____ are the indigenous people of New Zealand. They had been long suffering from unfair treatment after Europeans started to immigrate into the country. They were forced to use English. Also, their lifestyle was westernized, which led their unique culture to start fading away. However, after the WWⅡ, people in New Zealand began to think that they should do something to preserve their culture. Now their language and English are the official languages of New Zealand. New Zealand shows a good example of 2)_____ between different peoples.

©Somakram | Dreamstime.com

2) In the 20th century, 3)_____ had difficulty living in the US. Bus seating is a good example of their surroundings of that time. They could sit in a limited area on buses, though white people could use any seats in a bus. This situation can be categorized as 4)_____ against them.

©Science History Images | Alarmy Stock Photo

3) In the Edo period, Japan made itself isolated from other countries. The governors did this because they thought it was easier to rule their country with limited contact with other nations. In particular, they tried to eliminate 5)_____ from Japan. Many people were killed by the governors, so some people who didn't want to give up their religion decided to hide underground and pray for God. This policy can be categorized as the 6)_____ from their country.

﨑津教会

4 Reading graphs & charts 1

Refugee admission or recognition 難民受入と認定

CD1-08
↓ 008

Task 7 ▸ Fill in the blanks

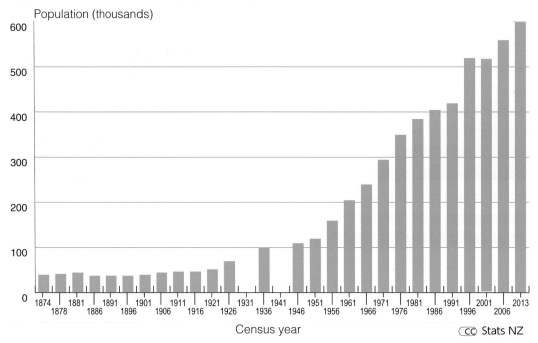

Maori population, 1874-2013 Censuses

Population (thousands)

Census year · CC Stats NZ

This bar graph shows the number of 1)_____ people living in New Zealand. They are indigenous people in the country. The number did not change so much from 1874 to 1916. However, it gradually started to 2)_____ in 1921, and the population in 2013 was about 3)_____ times larger than that in 1936. This research was not conducted in 1931 and 4)_____, so the numbers for those years are uncertain.

Task 8 ▸ Do research and discuss

1) Why did the population of Maori start to increase?
2) Do you think it is hard to live with indigenous people?
3) Do you know about the indigenous people called the Ainu in Japan? How are they doing now?

5 Reading graphs & charts 2

Muslims in the US   アメリカ合衆国のイスラム

Task 9 ▸ Fill in the blanks

D1-09
009

US Muslims Concerned about Their Place in Society

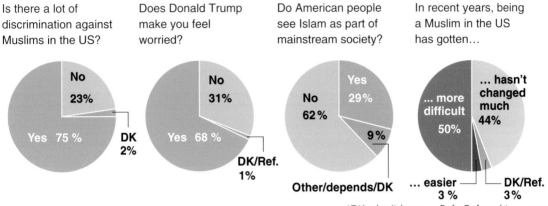

Is there a lot of discrimination against Muslims in the US?

Does Donald Trump make you feel worried?

Do American people see Islam as part of mainstream society?

In recent years, being a Muslim in the US has gotten…

No **23%** Yes **75 %** DK **2%**

No **31%** Yes **68 %** DK/Ref. **1%**

Yes **29%** No **62 %** Other/depends/DK **9%**

… **more difficult** **50%** … **hasn't changed much** **44%** … **easier** **3 %** DK/Ref. **3%**

*DK=don't know   Ref.=Refused to answer

These pie charts show how 1)_____ feel about their life in the US in 2017. The first chart shows 2)_____ % of Muslims feel a lot of discrimination against them. The second one shows that 3)_____ % of them are upset by the US President. The third one shows that only 4)_____ % of them feel that they are a part of mainstream society. The last one shows that half of them feel that being a Muslim is more 5)_____ than before. These results may suggest the US policy against Muslims.

Task 10 ▸ Do research and discuss

1) Do you think that it is reasonable to ban Muslims from entering your own country?
2) Do you think there is discrimination against Muslims in your own country?
3) Look at the graph below. Does President Trump's policy on Muslims have a positive effect on America's economic growth?

US GDP Growth Rate

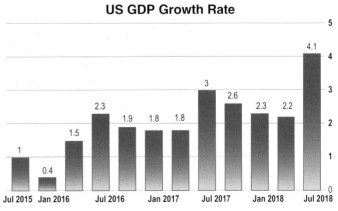

Jul 2015 Jan 2016 Jul 2016 Jan 2017 Jul 2017 Jan 2018 Jul 2018

1   0.4   1.5   2.3   1.9   1.8   1.8   3   2.6   2.3   2.2   4.1

23

CD1-10
↓ 010

Jane and Toshi are talking about people and places. What do you think about the underlined parts especially? Do you agree with their opinions?

J: Last Sunday when I went to Harajuku to buy a new bag, I felt worried. There were many more non-Japanese people walking on the street than ever before.

T: Do you mean that you want fewer people from other countries to visit Japan?

J: I am just worried. 1) If they increase in Japan, it will be a more inconvenient place to live.

T: Do you mean Japanese people can't live together with them?

J: 2) If more non-Japanese people come to live in Japan, their lifestyle will become the mainstream of the society.

T: Okay, let's talk about China towns, for example. There are more and more China towns around the world. Do you feel the towns affect the local culture in a negative way?

J: I'm not sure, but Japanese people are not used to interacting with people with certain religions, such as Islam or Judaism.

T: Well, that is a difficult topic. It is true that humans have had a lot of religious wars around the world. 3) There may also be a risk that immigrants will fight with each other in Japan because of their differences in religions.

J: Oh, I really hope that kind of thing will never happen in Japan. 4) I wonder if we can solve such religious conflicts.

T: I'm not sure, but I hope there will be no religious and ethnic wars.

Task 11 ▸ What do you think about people and places? Do you think Japan should welcome more different nationalities?

Be a Good Consumer

買い物上手になる

1 Brainstorming

Look at these pictures. Aren't these products fascinating? Some people say that buying these things is not good. Why? They also say, "Shopping is voting." What does this mean? Let's think about it.

Warm up Talk to your classmate(s), and then listen to the explanation.

Task 1 Listen to the explanation and fill in the blanks

01-11
011

We enjoy shopping to buy many different things. The 1)_____ of products makes us feel that shopping is fun. However, buying some products means that you've made an ethically bad 2)_____. Palm oil is often used to produce lipsticks. To make palm oil, a lot of 3)_____ are cut down and made into fields for palm trees. In the forest there are animals and insects which can't 4)_____ in the palm trees. Buying lipsticks with palm oil is like pushing away those animals and insects. Moreover, buying 5)_____ eggs means that you agree with persecuting chickens. In some of the chicken farms in Japan, chickens are kept in a very 6)_____ cage. When they try to move their wings, they often break their bones. Also, they have a lot of 7)_____ because of being packed in a small box. Some of them suffer from diseases because of the 8)_____, but the farmers don't treat them. If they find such chickens, they just kill them. This cruel way of breeding is banned in 9)_____, but many of the chicken farms in Japan choose this breeding method. Buying these products means that you agree with the 10)_____ of the people or organization that have made the goods.

Task 2 Do shadowing

01-12
012

Task 3 Talk in pairs

1) Have you ever bought any of the products mentioned above?
2) How can you avoid buying such products?
3) Try to find things that contain palm oil.

2 Word info 1

Task 4 Quiz

Q1 Which best describes mass production?

a) Taro works in a sushi restaurant. One day his restaurant was very busy at lunch time, so he and his coworker made a lot of sushi on that day.

b) Jane works at a bank. Every day she has to count many coins by using a coin counter. Without the machine, she would have to spend a lot of time on just counting the number of coins.

©Celil Kirnapci/Shutterstock.com

c) Jack works for a publishing company. Now he can print out so many newspapers just by pressing the button of a printer. However, in the past, a lot of people were needed to print out newspapers.

Q2 Who is a craftsman?

a) Jane grows vegetables in her field. She works six days a week, taking a rest on Sundays. She sells her vegetables directly at local farmers' markets. Although she can't earn a lot of money, she is satisfied with her slow lifestyle.

©Fotoluni nate | Dreamstime.com

b) Tom makes traditional products in Mexico. He has worked this way for more than 20 years. Although he can't earn a lot of money, he is proud of contributing to preserving his own country's tradition. He makes the products by hand, so he can't make a large quantity at one time.

©Ulita | Dreamstime.com

c) Edward is a teacher. He has worked at his school for more than 10 years. Since he is kind, diligent, and good at teaching, he is respected by many students and his co-workers. His school is a private school.

©Monkey Business Images | Dreamstime.com

Task 5 Discuss in pairs

Which person mentioned above do you like? Why do you think so? Do you want to have a slow life or have a fast life?

3 Word info 2

Task 6 Fill in the blanks with the words in the box. What do these words mean? Explain them to your classmate.

eco-friendly   industrialization   fair trade   fast fashion   consumer taste

1) In the old days people didn't use machines to make products. They made what they needed by hand, so the production was not effective. However, after they started to produce by using machines, they could begin to make many more products in a shorter time. This process is called 1)_____ . Through this change, many new business models were born. 2)_____ is one of them. By producing the same kind of clothing with machines at one time, the prices of fast fashion products are much lower than other counterparts.

2) Now more and more people buy things from an ethical perspective. Electric cars are more popular than before because they are 3)_____ . More people choose to buy 4)_____ chocolate, although it is more expensive than other chocolate. These people are called "ethical consumers." This is a new trend of 5)_____ , so companies try to make goods that can meet the demand.

©nd3000/iStockphoto.com

4 Reading graphs & charts 1

Mass production 大量生産

CD1-13
↓ 013

Task 7 ▶ Fill in the blanks

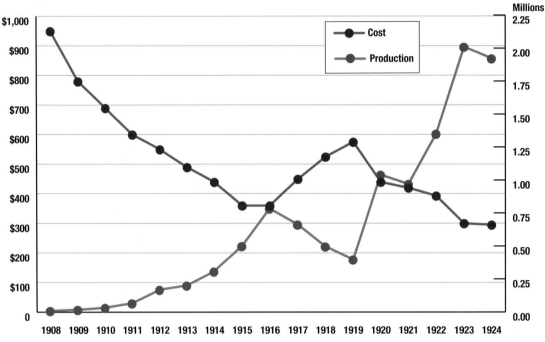

(Source: Case File of Henry Ford, Committee on Science and the Arts)

This graph shows how many cars were produced each year by Ford, one of the biggest motor companies in the world, and how much it cost to make one car in a specific year. In 1908 the company produced quite 1)_____ amounts of cars. At that time the cost for production was very high. But in 2)_____, when Ford produced about 0.75 million cars, its production cost dropped by more than half, less than 3)_____ dollars. The cost sounds quite low, but one dollar at that time was 4)_____ to about 20 dollars in 2006. In 1924, the cost was below 300 dollars when the company made almost two 5)_____ cars. This graph may show that people can get goods in a low 6)_____ when a company makes a lot of specific products at one time.

Task 8 ▶ Do research and discuss

1) Is mass production good or bad? What products are mass produced?
2) Car sharing is more and more popular in Japan. In the future, do you want to have your own car, or share a car with others?

5 Reading graphs & charts 2

Traditional handicraft vs. industrialization 伝統工芸品と工業化

Task 9 Fill in the blanks

01-14
014

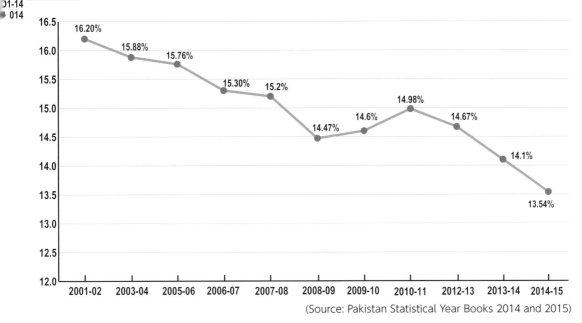

(Source: Pakistan Statistical Year Books 2014 and 2015)

This graph shows the percentage of people who work for traditional handicraft in Pakistan. The percentage keeps on going down from 2001-2002 to 1)_____. Although it pops up a little from 2008-2009 to 2)_____, the percentage starts to go down again from 2010-2011 to 3)_____. The research shows that the percentage didn't stop declining because of industrialization. Now people can make a lot of new 4)_____ by using machines in a 5)_____ price, although traditional handicraft products are supposed to be made with human hands, resulting in 6)_____ prices than machine-made products. Also, the design can't be changed easily because the craftwork is the country's tradition, while the 7)_____ of machine-made products can be easily 8)_____ according to the consumers' tastes which are changing more frequently than before. The number of 9)_____ is decreasing in Pakistan.

Task 10 Do research and discuss

1) Should the government of Pakistan protect this traditional handicraft?
2) Can traditional handicraft and industrialization coexist in one country?
3) Find similar problem(s) in Japan.

6 Discussion & presentation

CD1-15
◆ 015

Jane and Paul are talking about many kinds of cheap products around the world. What do you think about the underlined parts especially? Do you agree with their opinions?

J: Hi, Paul. You're wearing a nice jacket! Where did you buy it?

P: I bought it at a fast fashion store. There we can buy jackets for low prices. 1) <u>We can wear fast fashion clothes for a long time, so fast fashion must be eco-friendly.</u>

J: Well, there are sacrifices made to sell such inexpensive products. Have you heard about that?

P: Oh, yes. Most fast-fashion companies have factories in developing countries. Some women are forced to work in factories to make clothes for 3 dollars a day.

J: That's true, and I sometimes wonder if it is good to buy clothing at fast fashion shops.

P: Should we give up purchasing clothes at low prices?

J: That might be for the best. You know most coffee beans are made in developing countries as well. Coffee farmers can't make a lot of money by growing the beans.

P: That means 2) <u>coffee farmers' lifestyles are sacrificed for our convenience of buying coffee at a low price. That sounds totally unfair.</u>

J: To solve this problem, some companies have started a fair trade coffee system. If this fair trade system is applied, coffee farmers can receive appropriate salaries.

P: 3) <u>If we don't want to sacrifice anything or anyone for our shopping, we need to have a lot of money to buy fair trade products.</u>

J: Maybe that is the true price of the products.

Task 11 ▶ **What do you think about cheap goods? Do you buy your clothes at a fast fashion store? Do you agree with fair trade?**

Unit 4

Learn about Food, Culture and Society

食物、文化、社会について知る

1 Brainstorming

Look at these pictures. There are a variety of meals on the tables. Now you must be hungry, right? What makes each meal different? Why are there many kinds of meals in the world? In this unit we are going to focus on food, culture and society.

Warm up Talk to your classmate(s), and then listen to the explanation.

Task 1 Listen to the explanation and fill in the blanks

1-16
016 There are many kinds of 1)_____ in the world. In most cases, people who believe in a specific religion may be given restrictions on their lifestyles. For example, Hindus need to 2)_____ the cattle and are not allowed to kill them. The restrictions often have a great influence on the 3)_____ that can be eaten. Muslims are prohibited from eating 4)_____ because their religion tells them that pigs are impure animals. Buddhists don't eat any 5)_____ because they think that all life in the world is equal. In order to get protein, Buddhists use 6)_____ beans instead of eating meat, so their diet is very healthy. Some Christians don't drink 7)_____. However, there is an exception. Many Christians drink 8)_____ wine because their Bible says that red wine is the 9)_____ of the Son of God, so it is a sacred drink.

Task 2 Do shadowing

1-17
017
Task 3 Talk in pairs

1) Which food restriction is most interesting to you?
2) Which food restriction is most difficult for you?
3) Is it necessary to set up any food restrictions on your eating habits?

2 Word info 1

Task 4 ▸ Quiz

Q1 Which is which?

Vegetarians don't eat any meat due to healthy, environmental, ethical, religious or economic reasons. There are three types of vegetarians: **1) lacto-ovo vegetarians, 2) lacto-vegetarians, and 3) vegans. Which people are they?**

a) people who eat only plant foods
b) people who don't eat meat, seafood or eggs, but eat dairy foods and plant foods
c) people who don't eat meat or seafood, but eat dairy foods and plant foods

Q2 Which type of vegetarian is the following person?

a) A likes eating vegetables. He especially likes to eat slices of tomato with fresh cheese. His favorite cheese is mozzarella, made from cow's milk. He never eats meat because of his religion.
b) B doesn't like to eat carbohydrates because she thinks they are not good for her health. In particular, at night she never eats carbohydrates because it makes her fatter. She eats a lot of vegetables and meats to get necessary nutrition.
c) C's eating habit is very primitive. She never buys anything at a supermarket or eats anything at a restaurant. She finds what she needs in nature and gets what she wants to eat in the field or in the sea. She believes that food from nature is the healthiest.
d) D follows Buddhism. He agrees that all living things are equal, so he doesn't eat any meat. He even doesn't eat eggs or drink milk. He just eats vegetables to get necessary nutrition. He is proud of his choice.

©Paul K wan/Dreamstime.com   ©Celil Kirnapci/Shutterstock.com

Task 5 ▸ Discuss in pairs

1) What do you think about vegetarians? Which type of vegetarians would you like to be?
2) Some people in Japan have tried to diet to lose weight. Have you ever tried to change your eating habits?
3) What type of eating habit do you have?

3 Word info 2

Task 6 ▶ Fill in the blanks with the words in the box.

> eating habits   obesity   table manners
>
> utensils   slaughterhouse   blood pressure

1) More and more people in developed countries
eat too much. As a result many people have a
health problem called 1)_____. If people
have this condition, they are more likely to get
health problems such as high 2)_____.
The governments try to solve this problem by
introducing new health checks or food regulation
systems, but in most cases, this problem can't be
solved completely. People should change their
3)_____ if they want to stay away
from this problem.

©Delpixart/iStockphoto.com

2) 4)_____ is a place where cows, pigs
or chickens are killed for food. Most people don't
want to go to such a cruel place, so it is usually far
away from the center of a city. But we shouldn't
forget that most of the meats we eat are
processed in this place.

©Wicki58/iStockphoto.com

3) Eating habits vary from culture to culture. The
5)_____ we use and how to use them are also part of
culture. For example, we use chopsticks, forks, knives, and
spoons, and we often eat food by hand. In addition, place
settings are part of eating culture. Whether you eat at home
or at a restaurant, good 6)_____ make for
a more pleasant meal.

Vegan ビーガン

Task 7 Fill in the blanks

CD1-18
⬇ 018

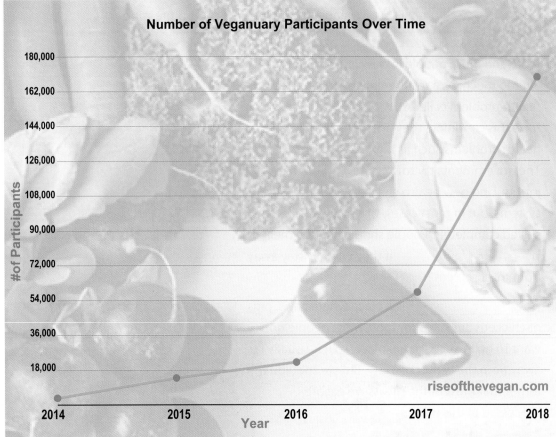

Number of Veganuary Participants Over Time

riseofthevegan.com

Veganuary is a charity organization in the UK that helps people to try vegan cuisine by introducing good vegan restaurants and good food recipes for vegans. This graph shows that the number of its 1)_____ increased greatly in 2018. The number of its participants was just about 2)_____ in 2016, but it increased by about 3)_____ in 2017. The biggest growth occurred in 4)_____, from about 54,000 to more than 5)_____. The increase shows that more and more people are interested in a vegan lifestyle.

Task 8 Do research and discuss

1) What are vegans?
2) What do you think about the Veganuary campaign?
3) Are there any vegetarian people around you?

5 Reading graphs & charts 2

Obesity 肥満

Task 9 Fill in the blanks

D1-19
019

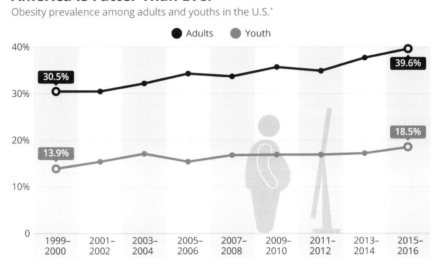

America Is Fatter Than Ever
Obesity prevalence among adults and youths in the U.S.*

● Adults   ● Youth

30.5%

39.6%

13.9%

18.5%

| 1999–2000 | 2001–2002 | 2003–2004 | 2005–2006 | 2007–2008 | 2009–2010 | 2011–2012 | 2013–2014 | 2015–2016 |

* Adults aged 20 and over and youth aged 2–19 years.
@StatistaCharts   Source: Centers For Control And Prevention

statista

This graph shows the 1)_____ rates in America. For adults the percentage was just about 2)_____ in 1999-2000. However, the percentage gradually became higher and higher, and topped in 3)_____ . For youth the percentage was about 13.9 in 4)_____ . The number dropped a little in 5)_____ , but after that the percentage consistently increased, and topped in 6)_____ . The graph suggests that more and more Americans are getting 7)_____ , having a risk of suffering from serious diseases such as heart attack. Some steps should be taken to solve this problem.

Task 10 Do research and discuss

> The State of New York found out that the cause of this obesity problem is overconsumption of sugar. The mayor introduced a tax on sugar, trying to stop people from using a lot of sugar.

1) Why are Americans becoming fatter than ever before?
2) Do you think this is a good approach? What do you think about it?

6 Discussion & presentation

CD1-20
⬇ 020

Sakura and Paul are talking about eating culture around the world. What do you think about the underlined parts especially? Do you agree with their opinions?

P: Hi, Sakura. I'm not so fine, actually. In the morning my teacher showed us the pictures taken in a slaughterhouse that some vegans used to stop people from eating meat. They were so disgusting.

S: You really look unwell, Paul.

P: Yeah, but I just have no appetite.

S: 1) Pictures can help us think about problems very seriously, because they capture the real situation where problems exist.

P: Uh, I know what you mean, but the pictures were too shocking! Now I don't want to eat anything. I should be a vegan.

S: 2) If you say they are too shocking and you don't want to see them, that means you will have no chance to see the harsh reality in the world.

P: Well, actually that's true. My teacher also told us that some vegans started to attack people who eat meat. People around the world should respect each other's different eating habits.

S: Absolutely. I remember the sad news of a Japanese food company. They falsely sold Muslims a seasoning including pork. But pork was not on the list of its ingredients. They must have been very upset and very sad. 3) If the company had been more aware and respectful of their eating habits, the problem could have been solved.

P: We should remember that diversity makes the world more interesting and enjoyable. Otherwise, we would have to eat the same kind of food every day! That would be so boring.

Task 11 ▸ What do you think about different eating habits?

Have Better Lifestyles in Different Cultures

文化に応じたより良い生活スタイルを送る

1 Brainstorming

Look at the pictures. They show nature and life in Bhutan. Do you know where Bhutan is located? Some people say that Bhutan is one of the happiest countries in the world. Gross National Happiness (GNH) is a philosophy in Bhutan. What do you think about GNH?

Warm up Talk to your classmate(s), and then listen to the explanation.

D1-21
021
Task 1 Listen to the explanation and fill in the blanks

"If the government cannot create 1)_____ for the people, there is no purpose for the government." This is what Bhutan's king said in 1972. Based on this idea, the government started to conduct a very famous 2)_____ called Gross National Happiness or GNH. When they conduct the survey, they identify some 3)_____ that influence happiness. Bhutan is friendly to the environment, so about 50 % of the country is protected as a national 4)_____. By doing so, its trees or 5)_____ can be safe from environmental destruction such as deforestation. Many people there believe that protecting nature can lead to their happiness. Another factor that they think makes people happy is cultural 6)_____. They think it is important to preserve and promote their cultural traditions. One example of this is their 7)_____ garment or clothing, which is called Gho or Kira. However, some people disagree with the idea that Bhutan is the 8)_____ country in the world.

D1-22
022
Task 2 Do shadowing

Task 3 Talk in pairs

1) What is an important factor for your own happiness?
2) Which is more important, Gross National Product or Gross National Happiness?
3) Is it possible to measure the degree of people's happiness?

2 Word info 1

Task 4 ▶ Quiz

Q1 Which does 'maternity leave' mean? Why do you think so?

a) A woman quits working after pregnancy, without any promise of returning to a workplace.

b) A woman asks someone to take care of one's baby and start to work again after giving birth.

c) A woman gets paid leave during the period of pregnancy and after giving birth.

Q2 Which best describes a slow life? Why do you think so?

a) Ryo lives in the countryside. He is a junior high school teacher. He needs to be at school very early in the morning. In addition, he has many things to do, so he usually leaves school at 8 pm. Because he is often exhausted, he does almost nothing at home, except for his housework. His lifestyle sounds hard, but he likes his job and enjoys his life.

b) Nana likes music, gardening, and playing sports. As she wants to spend a lot of time on her hobbies, she just works from 10 to 4. Sometimes her parents say she is lazy to focus on her hobbies. She knows she could earn more money if she worked longer, but she thinks that kind of lifestyle would be meaningless for her.

c) Ken wants to make a difference. He likes to pursue his full potential at his job. Every time he gets promoted, he thinks that he is an important person in his office and feels content with his lifestyle. In order to achieve his full potential at his job, he thinks taking a rest is also important, but on days-off he always studies about something important for his job.

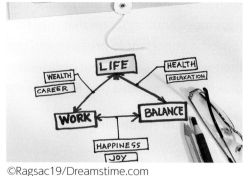

©Ragsac19/Dreamstime.com

Task 5 ▶ Discuss in pairs

1) What is the benefit of getting maternity leave?

2) Which is better for you, a slow life or a fast life?

3 Word info 2

Task 6 Fill in the blanks with the words in the box.

> burn-out   days-off   paid holiday   30
>
> preference   work-life balance

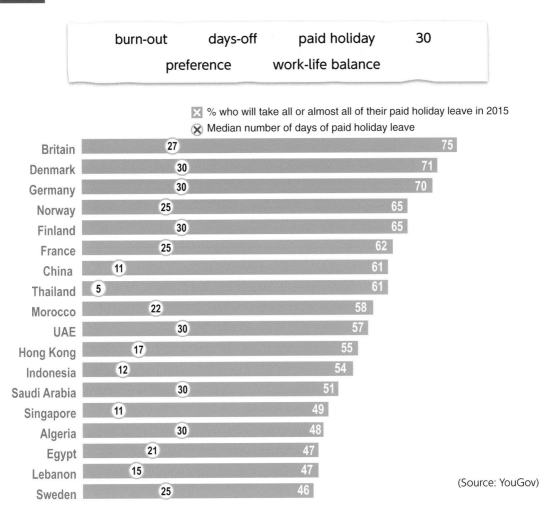

☒ % who will take all or almost all of their paid holiday leave in 2015
⊗ Median number of days of paid holiday leave

Country	Median days	% who take
Britain	27	75
Denmark	30	71
Germany	30	70
Norway	25	65
Finland	30	65
France	25	62
China	11	61
Thailand	5	61
Morocco	22	58
UAE	30	57
Hong Kong	17	55
Indonesia	12	54
Saudi Arabia	30	51
Singapore	11	49
Algeria	30	48
Egypt	21	47
Lebanon	15	47
Sweden	25	46

(Source: YouGov)

If you work in Denmark for one year, you can have about 1)_____ holidays in the year. During the periods you can receive your salary. This period is called 2)_____. You have the right of getting paid holidays in Denmark, but Japanese workers take only half of them on average, according to a survey conducted by YouGov, a global public opinion and data company. Another survey shows that some Japanese people feel guilt for taking 3)_____. The attitude clearly shows that people in Japan underestimate the importance of 4)_____. It is important to pursue both achievement and enjoyment in life. But just seeking achievement at a job, people tend to forget pursuing the enjoyment of life, which can lead to more serious problems such as 5)_____ or suicide. If you think you can enjoy life by working long hours, that's your 6)_____. However, you need to be careful not to impose your idea onto others.

Paternity leave 男性育児休暇

Task 7 Fill in the blanks

CD1-23
↓ 023 **Where Fathers Receive The Most Paternity Leave**
Weeks of paid leave and average payment related to national earnings in 2014

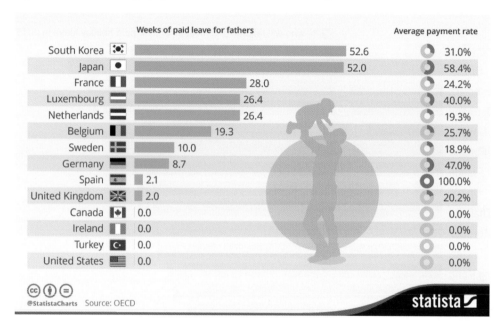

	Weeks of paid leave for fathers		Average payment rate
South Korea		52.6	31.0%
Japan		52.0	58.4%
France		28.0	24.2%
Luxembourg		26.4	40.0%
Netherlands		26.4	19.3%
Belgium	19.3		25.7%
Sweden	10.0		18.9%
Germany	8.7		47.0%
Spain	2.1		100.0%
United Kingdom	2.0		20.2%
Canada	0.0		0.0%
Ireland	0.0		0.0%
Turkey	0.0		0.0%
United States	0.0		0.0%

@StatistaCharts Source: OECD

statista

This graph shows how many days for paternity leave each father can have in various countries. Paternity leave means that fathers can receive paid 1)_____ for taking care of their babies when the babies are very little. This graph is extracted from an OECD report. As the graph shows, 2)_____ offers the most days-off to fathers, following 3)_____ in second place. Those two countries offer many days-off, but very few of the fathers make use of the system. On the other hand, in 4)_____, which offers 10 weeks of paid leave for fathers, more than 80 % of them take paternity leave. Fathers usually get less payment from a company during paternity leave, but they can receive 100 % of their salary payment in 5)_____.

Task 8 Do research and discuss

1) Do you think paternity leave is a good system?
2) Do you want to take paternity leave or want your husband to take it in the future?
3) Why do many men not take paternity leave in Japan and South Korea?

©Pojoslaw/Dreamstime.com

5 Reading graphs & charts 2

Homework 宿題

Task 9 Fill in the blanks

01-24
024 **The Countries Where Kids Do The Most Homework**

Hours of homework per week in selected countries (15-year old students)

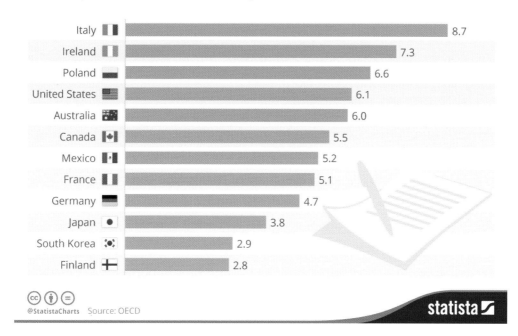

@StatistaCharts   Source: OECD

statista

This graph shows the amount of time students in each country do homework per week. According to the graph, in 1)_____ students have the most homework from school. 2)_____ comes second, followed by 3)_____. Students in Finland have the least homework, 4)_____ hours per week. This graph doesn't necessarily mean that students in Italy study the hardest in the world. In 5)_____, where students spend 3.8 hours on homework a week, schools finish at 4 to 6 pm, but most students go to juku in the evening.

Task 10 Do research and discuss

1) What time do you leave school in Japan? How about students in other countries?
2) Which school system do you like among the countries in the graph?
3) Do you think schools should give more homework to students?
4) What kind of homework is good for students?

6 Discussion & presentation

CD1-25
025

Paul and Xiaoxue are talking about different lifestyles around the world. What do you think about the underlined parts especially? Do you agree with their opinions?

P: Now I'm doing job hunting. I'm looking for a workplace which gives me at least 120 days-off in a year. In Germany people get 144 days-off on average.

X: Oh, you mean you want to sustain your work-life balance? 1) I think the easiest way to achieve your idea is to go to the countryside and be a farmer.

P: Actually, I don't want to live in the countryside. It is inconvenient. There are often no shopping malls to hang out. I don't like it.

X: 2) It might be impossible to achieve a slow life in the city.

P: Even when living in the city, we can be eco-friendly by consuming less. Using a lot of electricity is bad for the environment, because it emits CO_2 into the atmosphere.

X: That's true. According to Maslow's Hierarchy of Needs, you can be happier if you try to achieve your full potential. Getting enough rest and living in the city is your preference.

P: Thanks. I need to think deeply about my career again. But in reality, many people in the city like to consume a lot, I guess.

X: Education is a key to the problem. We need to learn how important it is to reduce, reuse, and recycle materials.

P: Do you mean people in the city need to change their lifestyles? That's not fair.

X: No, that's not what I mean. What I mean is that sustainability is most important. 3) If our lifestyle hinders the sustainability of a society, we need to change our lifestyle. Nothing should be sacrificed for the development of society. We need to seek new ways to achieve both economic growth and work-life balance.

Task 11 ▶ What do you think about different lifestyles? Do you want to live in the city or in the countryside?

Unit 6 — Be an Intercultural Traveler

互いの文化を理解する旅行者となる

1 Brainstorming

Look at the picture. Do you know what this is? It's the Kaminari-mon gate, one of the biggest entrance gates leading to the Senso-ji Temple in Tokyo. As you can see in the picture, it is always crowded around the gate with tourists from around the world, as well as domestic tourists. Many people like traveling, but have you ever thought about why people travel?

写真：長田洋平 / アフロ

Warm up Talk to your classmate(s), and then listen to the passage.

Task 1 ▸ Listen to the passage and fill in the blanks

1-26
026

Do you like traveling? Now you can take cars, buses, trains, ships and airplanes, and you are able to enjoy traveling not only in your own country but also in other countries. Can you quickly answer the question, "Why do you travel?" Here are some answers to the question. First, traveling makes you feel happy. You can see beautiful mountains, 1)_____ buildings, and fantastic 2)_____. There are many things that make you feel interested and excited. Second, if you travel, you can see what you have never seen before, which becomes an intellectual 3)_____. Once you are stimulated, you may want to know more about another country and start doing some research on it. Third, you can see your own culture from a different 4)_____. For example, in Japan it is quite usual that you are not 5)_____ to talk on the phone in trains, but that is not the case in other countries. Once you know that, you may feel it strange that you should refrain from talking on the phone in trains.

Task 2 ▸ Do shadowing

1-27
027

Task 3 ▸ Talk in pairs

1) Do you like traveling? Where is your favorite tourist spot?
2) Is there any other reason for traveling? What are some advantages of traveling?

2　Word info 1

Task 4 ▸ Quiz

Q1　Which do you practice? Are there any other traditional behaviors you practice?

a) New Year's visit to a shrine or a temple（初詣）

b) New Year's cards（年賀状）

c) Bean throwing festival（節分）

d) The Doll Festival or Girls' Day（ひな祭り）

e) The vernal (autumnal) equinox week / visiting the family grave（彼岸、お墓詣り）

f) The year-end general cleaning（年末大掃除）

g) Others（　　　　　　）

Q2　Which best describes the following Japanese goods?

> Yukata　Kokeshi　Wagashi　Matcha　Sake　Furoshiki

a) It refers to traditional Japanese sweets which people enjoy with green tea.

b) It is traditionally often referred to Japanese rice wine that is made by fermenting rice.

c) It is a garment which functions as a quick way to cover the body and absorb remaining moisture. You wear it after a bath.

d) It is a traditional wrapping cloth, which can transform into various shapes depending on what it is used to wrap.

e) It is a fine type of green tea which is made by taking young tea leaves and grinding them into a bright green powder.

f) It is a traditional wooden doll and has been a valuable part of Japanese folk handicraft.

Task 5 ▸ Discuss in pairs

1) How many festivals do you know about? Which festival do you like most?

2) What kind of gifts or presents would you take with you in visiting people in other countries?

3 Word info 2

Task 6 Fill in the blanks with the following words. What do you think about these tourism words?

> concierge   overbooking   travel agent

1) _____ is the practice to sell more airline or hotel tickets than the actual number of people that can be accommodated. It often aims to avoid empty seats or rooms due to no-shows.

2) The _____ is a person who supports your tours and activities in a hotel lobby. He or she might also handle restaurant reservations, booking theater tickets, and other arrangements for you.

3) The _____ is a professional who helps travelers to plan vacations. As a tour or activity provider, he or she is engaged in selling and arranging tours or trips, transportation, and accommodations for travelers.

Task 7 Match the related words in A and B, and choose 3 factors you regard as important in planning a trip.

A

a) distance
b) sightseeing or scenery
c) accommodation
d) cultural and historical spots
e) travel costs and prices
f) cuisine
g) entertainment and attractions
h) climate and geography

B

1) how much money you have to pay
2) local dishes
3) mountains, lakes, forests, coasts, etc.
4) hotels, inns, B&B, etc.
5) concerts, musicals, casinos, amusement parks, etc.
6) how much time you need to get to the destination
7) castles, temples, mosques, museums, ruins, etc.
8) temperature, precipitation, humidity, sunshine duration, etc.

Inbound and outbound tourists in Japan
訪日（外国人）旅行者と海外（日本人）旅行者

CD1-28
↓ 028

Task 8 ▶ Fill in the blanks

Trends in Visitor Arrivals to Japan and Japanese Overseas Travelers by Year

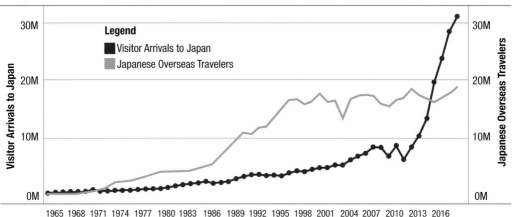

(Source: Japan National Travel Organization JNTO)

This graph shows the number of inbound and outbound tourists in Japan. In 2000, the annual number of foreign tourists who came to Japan was about 1)_____ million, but after that the number has been increasing continuously. In particular, the growth of inbound tourists has been exponential since 2010, and the number of foreign tourists reached 31 million in 2)_____. On the other hand, the number of Japanese tourists increased very rapidly between 3)_____ and 4)_____, but these days it has been rather stable, staying between 5)_____ and 6)_____ million.

Task 9 ▶ Do research and discuss

1) What are the causes of the increase of inbound and outbound tourists?
2) The Japanese government aims at accepting 60 million inbound tourists in 2030. Do you think this will be possible? Why or why not?

©boana/iStickphoto.com

5 Reading graphs & charts 2

Countries that attract tourists ツーリストを魅了する国

Task 10 ▸ **Fill in the blanks**

01-29
029

These graphs show the country rankings of the number of international tourists and the receipts of international tourism in 2017. As for the number of international tourists, 1)_____ went up to 8th place from 10th in 2016, while 2)_____ stayed in 1st place in both years. The USA had fewer international tourists from other countries in 2017 than in 2016. However, the international tourists spent the highest amount of money in the US in 2017. They spent 3)_____ billion US dollars. The receipt was more than 4)_____ times as much as that in Spain, which was in second place (US$ 68 billion).

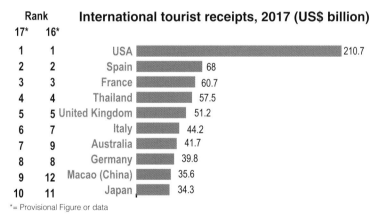

Rank

17*	16*	International tourist arrivals, 2017 (million)	
1	1	France	86.9
2	3	Spain	81.8
3	2	USA	76.9
4	4	China	60.7
5	5	Italy	58.3
6	8	Mexico	39.3
7	6	United Kingdom	37.7
8	10	Turkey	37.6
9	7	Germany	37.5
10	9	Thailand	35.4

*= Provisional Figure or data

Rank

17*	16*	International tourist receipts, 2017 (US$ billion)	
1	1	USA	210.7
2	2	Spain	68
3	3	France	60.7
4	4	Thailand	57.5
5	5	United Kingdom	51.2
6	7	Italy	44.2
7	9	Australia	41.7
8	8	Germany	39.8
9	12	Macao (China)	35.6
10	11	Japan	34.3

*= Provisional Figure or data

(Source: United Nations World Tourism Organization (UNWTO, 2018))

Task 11 ▸ **Do research and discuss**

1) Why is France the most popular destination among international tourists? What attracts tourists?

2) International tourists seem to use a lot of money in the US. What do they spend their money on? Why is the gap of the receipts so big between the US and Spain?

6 Discussion & presentation

CD1-30
↓ 030

Xiaoxue and Toshi are talking about Toshi's experiences about traveling. Let's think about the underlined parts with classmates.

X: Hi, Toshi. How was your summer vacation?

T: Hi, Xiaoxue. I visited Australia and Indonesia.

X: Wow, fantastic! How did you find those countries?

T: In Australia, I felt that people there thought highly of nature. They are trying very hard to save the wildlife including the animals that are becoming extinct.

X: I see. I know there are many rare animals like koalas, emus and cassowaries. 1) I think Japan should also be more aware of the issues of biodiversity.

T: That's true. I learned the animals are in danger due to the behavior of humans.

X: How about Indonesia?

T: I found a lot of cultural differences there. People pray five times a day, walk very slowly, and drive very roughly. Women wear hijab. 2) Japan is more of a mono-culture, so it may be boring.

X: That's interesting. Did you stay in Jakarta?

T: Yes, but I also visited the Borobudur Temple Compounds in Central Java. It's really magnificent, and I was just overwhelmed. However, the site is being damaged.

X: Damaged? Why?

T: Some tourists make scratches on the wall, and others throw garbage on the ground. Moreover, the cars and buses produce a lot of carbon monoxide fumes, which are likely to damage the Compounds.

X: That's too bad. 3) That means tourism may have both positive and negative effects on the sites.

©Marco taliani de Marchio/Dreamstime.com

©jukrae/Shutterstock.com

Task 12 ▸ What are the "positive" and "negative" effects that tourism has on the tourist spots? Choose one tourist spot, and do research about the positive and negative effects on the spot.

Unit 7

Cultivate Global Citizenship

地球市民感覚を培う

1 Brainstorming

Look at the picture. What is the information written on the globe? It says, "On March 11, 2011, The Great East Japan Earthquake Struck Japan". What happened in Japan on that day? How did the earthquake affect us? As global citizens, we need to learn about global issues and think about what we can do about them. Share your views about global citizenship.

Warm up Talk to your classmate(s), and then listen to the explanation.

Task 1 Listen to the explanation and fill in the blanks

1-31
031

Global citizens are those who are aware of the wider or expanding 1)_____ and understand their place in it. They can have an 2)_____ role in their community and work with others to make our society more 3)_____, fair and sustainable. UNESCO's Global Citizenship Education aims to encourage all 4)_____ to play active roles in building more 5)_____, tolerant, inclusive and secure societies. Global Citizenship Education has three conceptual dimensions: cognitive, socio-emotional and behavioral domains of learning. Cognitive domain of learning includes knowledge and 6)_____ skills. Socio-emotional domains of learning includes values, 7)_____ and social skills. Behavioral 8)_____ of learning mean conduct, performance, practical application and engagement.

Task 2 Do shadowing

1-32
032

Task 3 Talk in pairs

1) Have you heard about global citizenship before?
2) Do you agree with global citizenship education? Why do you think so?

2 Word info 1

Task 4 ▸ Quiz

Q1 Citizenship: What does it mean to you? Why do you think so?

  a) a feeling of belonging to a local community
  b) having the rights to residence, voting and employment
  c) people's affiliation with the nation and their duties in relation to it

Q2 Global competence: What does it mean to you? Why do you think so?

  a) having global knowledge, open-mindedness and intercultural communication skills
  b) having an open mind, and intercultural knowledge to communicate effectively outside your environment
  c) having knowledge of current events and second language competence

Q3 Global citizenship: Which case is most helpful for you to develop your global citizenship?

  a) migration and mobility
  b) a commitment to live responsibly by taking care of the earth and its inhabitants
  c) awareness of societal justice, nonviolence and democracy, environmental care, and North-South relations
  d) action toward local, state, national, and global community issues

Q4 Engagement: Which case is most helpful for you to be engaged in the world?

  a) watching global news on TV or the Internet
  b) reading international reports in newspaper
  c) talking with international students about global issues
  d) joining a study abroad or volunteering abroad program
  e) participating in a global internship or an international association

Task 5 ▸ Discuss in pairs

1) Do you want to be a global citizen? Or are you a global citizen already? Why or why not?
2) Do you believe study abroad would help develop your global citizenship? Why or why not?

3 Word info 2

Task 6 There are some practical steps that you can take to develop intercultural competence and global citizenship. Which of the following steps do you take? Choose your top 3, and explain why.

1) **Become more self-aware**

It is necessary to recognize your strength and weakness in order to communicate more effectively in the intercultural setting. For example, you can obtain more intercultural knowledge to respond to cultural difference.

2) **Observe and actively listen**

In intercultural situations, you need carefully observe the verbal and nonverbal behaviors of your communication partners. Be an active listener and avoid stereotyping.

3) **Cultivate openness**

Don't think your culture is always superior to others. Try to be open to receive new ideas and behaviors: for example, in regard to local cuisine, different communication styles, and host language.

4) **Display respect**

Express respect for others. It varies depending on the different cultural context. Verbal and nonverbal expressions of respect may work well in one context, but they may be inappropriate in others.

5) **Be empathetic but not sympathetic**

In intercultural interactions, be aware of your communication partner's needs and feelings, and empathize with their world views and situations. Empathetic behaviors include verbal expressions and nonverbal actions.

6) **Be patient**

Developing intercultural competence is a process of continuous transformation that never ends. Developing yourself as a global citizen is best viewed as a life-long process rather than a product.

(Source: Jackson, 2014)

Top 1	
Top 2	
Top 3	

4 Reading graphs & charts 1

Students' views of global citizenship 大学生にとって地球市民とは?

CD1-33
↓ 033

Fill in the blanks

	Total	Hungary	USA
Learn about other cultures	85	54	31
Learn foreign languages	81	73	8
Learn to respect local cultural variations	66	33	33
Communicate with people from different cultures	63	48	15
Travel globally	52	35	17
Be an active member of community	40	19	21
Learn that among other duties we have as individuals we have responsibilities that are transnational	38	19	19
Learn to abide by universal ethical standards	35	9	26
Learn to reconcile local practice with hypernorms	28	20	8
Become politically involved	23	12	11

*Figures indicate the number of students.

(Source: Goluberva, Wagner and Yakimowski (2016))

The table shows questionnaire results comparing university students' understanding of the concept of what it means to be a "global citizen" in 1)_____ and Hungary. You see some 2)_____ between responses on 7 of the 10 listed characteristics of being a 3)_____ citizen: learn about other cultures, learn 4)_____ languages, communicate with people from different cultures, 5)_____ globally, learn to abide by universal ethical standards, and learn to reconcile 6)_____ practices with hypernorms. 7)_____ students agree more strongly than US students that learning foreign languages is important for being a global citizen. The results also show that Hungarian students emphasize 8)_____ and communicative aspects of global citizenship while US students focus on 9)_____ and ethical aspects.

Task 8 Do research and discuss

1) Do you agree with Hungarian or US students? Which do you agree with most?
2) Do you share any characteristics of global citizenship with them?
3) What characteristic of global citizen is important to you?

5 Reading graphs & charts 2

Global citizenship poll 地球市民意識調査

Task 9 Fill in the blanks

01-34
034

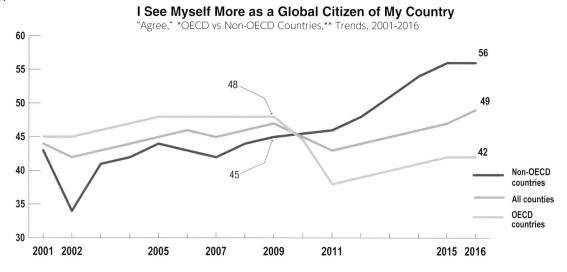

I See Myself More as a Global Citizen of My Country
"Agree," *OECD vs Non-OECD Countries,** Trends, 2001-2016

*"Stronlgy agree" plus "Somewhat agree"
**OECD countries include Canada, Chile, Germany, Mexico, Spain, UK, and USA; Non-OECD countries include Brazil, China, India, Indonesia, Kenya, Nigeria, and Russia. Not all countries were asked in all years.

(Source: GlobeScan)

GlobeScan, which is a public opinion research consultancy, conducted a poll among more than 20,000 people in OECD and non-OECD countries about global citizenship in 2016. For the first time in 15 years of tracking from 1)_____ to 2)_____ , findings indicate that nearly one in 3)_____ people (49 %) surveyed across 14 tracking countries see themselves more as 4)_____ citizens than citizens of their country. Among all the countries in 2016, the poll suggests more than half of the people see themselves more as global citizens than citizens of their 5)_____ . This is the first time this has happened since tracking began in 2001, and the results in 2016 are driven by strong increases. In 2009, views were 6)_____ across the two country groupings, with 48 % in seven OECD countries seeing themselves more as global citizens than national, and 45 % in seven non-OECD countries. By contrast in 2016, this trend in seven 7)_____ countries reached a high of 56 %, conversely in seven 8)_____ countries it dropped at 42 %.

Task 10 Do research and discuss

1) Do you see yourself more as a global citizen than a citizen of your country?
2) Ask your friend if he or she is a global citizen and why he or she thinks so.

6 Discussion & presentation

CD1-35
⬇ 035

Xiaoxue and Jane are talking about global citizenship. What do you think about the underlined parts especially? Do you agree with their opinions?

J: I think 1) global citizens are people who care less about nationalism and think more globally. They are interested in globalization. What do you think about global citizenship?

X: Well, to me, global citizens can speak at least two languages and are willing to communicate with people with different backgrounds. 2) Global citizens need to understand different cultures. Do you think you are a global citizen?

J: Yes, I think I am. People should have good communication skills and care about the whole world as well. How about you?

X: I'm sure I am a global citizen. I can speak Chinese, English and Japanese. I have many international friends on campus, and we usually learn together and attend many intercultural activities.

J: Wow, what kind of intercultural activities?

X: I often go to the International Communication Center. The staff organizes many activities, like a "Hanami" field trip in April, Language Lunches, and English Chat Club. I can make many international friends and learn about different cultures there.

J: That's great. I attended one field trip to Shanghai during summer vacation. 3) Shanghai is a really big international city. It was totally different from the image of China that I had before visiting. I visited a university in Shanghai and talked with Chinese students in English. Some Chinese students said they want to study in Japan. They are very interested in Japanese pop culture.

X: I am very glad you had a trip to Shanghai. You like Chinese food, right? Let's go to a Chinese restaurant together.

J: That sounds great! Let's go!

Task 11 ▸ What do you think about global citizenship? What kind of intercultural activities are you interested in?

Study the Education System

教育システムを知る

1　Brainstorming

The figure shows the education system in Finland. Can you find any differences between the Finnish system and the Japanese system? How different are they? Though tuition isn't shown in the chart, do you know how much you need to pay for tuition in Finland? It's very different from Japan.

Education system in Finland

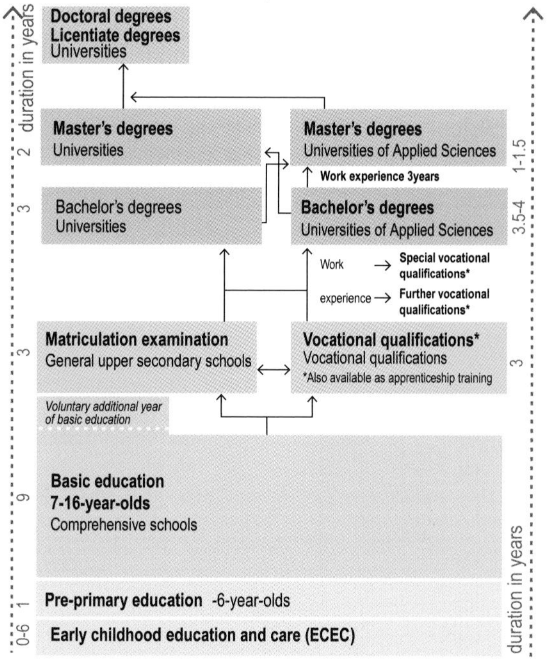

●Warm up　Talk to your classmate(s), and then listen to the passage.

1-36
036

Task 1 ▶ Listen to the passage and fill in the blanks

Schools and universities need a certain amount of revenue, because they need to pay salaries to their teachers and staff, buy teaching materials, pay for their 1)_____ , and so on. In many cases, the main source of their revenue is tuition. Then, who pays your tuition? It is said that there are three "tuition payers." The first source of tuition is the 2)_____ . For example, the government of Finland pays almost 100 % of your tuition for primary, secondary and 3)_____ education, as long as you are an EU citizen. The second "payer" is the parents. In most Asian countries such as Japan, China and Korea, the majority of university tuition is paid by them. The third source of tuition is the 4)_____ themselves. Many university students in the United States pay their own tuition by working part time, receiving 5)_____ or making student 6)_____ .

1-37
037

Task 2 ▶ Do shadowing

Task 3 ▶ Talk in pairs

1) Who pays your tuition?
2) Do you think your tuition is reasonable or expensive? Why?
3) Do you think Japan should make university tuition free?

2 Word info 1

Task 4 Match the words

1) primary education • • a) high school • • i) bachelor's degree
2) secondary education • • b) university/college • • ii) master's degree
3) tertiary education • • c) elementary school • • iii) doctor's degree
   • d) graduate school •

Task 5 Complete the chart of the education system in Japan, filling the blanks (A to F).

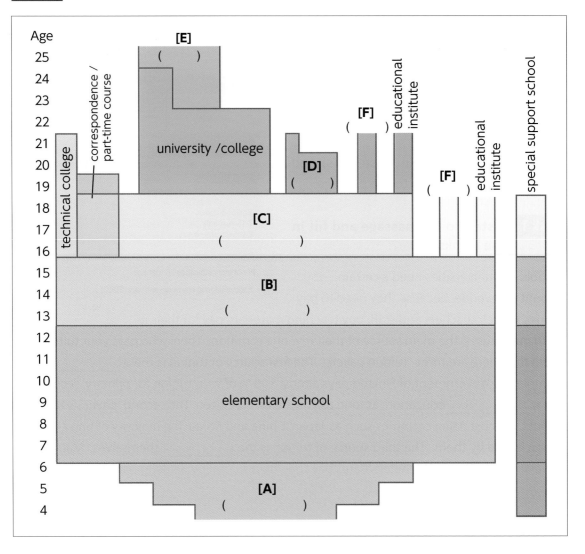

Task 6 Discuss in pairs

How much is your annual tuition? How much do you pay for educational expenses except for tuition?

3 Word info 2

Task 7 Quiz

Q1 You may hear the word 'public school' or 'public health,' for example. Which word is the opposite meaning of 'public'?

a) Today is an <u>official</u> holiday in Japan.

b) We will engage in an <u>educational</u> project.

c) You have to give an <u>informal</u> presentation.

d) We took <u>private</u> photos there.

Q2 'Expenditure' is money spent on something. Which word is the opposite of 'expenditure'?

a) There are some ways to increase <u>revenue</u> in your business.

b) Our school <u>budget</u> will be cut in half.

c) The <u>payment</u> of my tuition fees is completed.

d) You can find information about study <u>expenses</u>.

Q3 The dropout rate is relatively high in some countries. Which best describes the word of 'dropout'?

a) Kumi took a surgical operation and had been absent from college for three months, but now she enjoys going to college.

b) Yoshio has to work part time after school, because his father has lost his job.

c) Koichi was not able to get along with other students very well, and decided to quit school.

d) Yukiko is not good at math, and failed the mathematics course last year.

Q4 The enrollment rate is one of the important indexes for understanding the educational situation in a certain country. Which word's meaning is similar to the word 'enrollment'?

a) Bill took three <u>entrance</u> examinations of different universities, and passed all of them.

b) Becky graduated from university last year, but the monthly <u>payment</u> for her student loan has been a great burden on her life now.

c) Kathy once quit university due to sickness, but now she is thinking of <u>restarting</u> university.

d) In March, you can see a lot of female university students walking in *Kimono* and *Hakama* to attend their <u>graduation</u> ceremonies.

©Reinis Bigacs | Dreamstime.com

Expenditure on educational institutions 教育機関への支出

Task 8 ▸ Fill in the blanks

CD1-38
⬇ 038

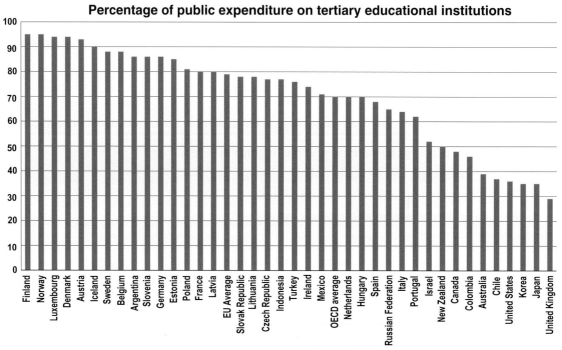

Percentage of public expenditure on tertiary educational institutions

(Source: OECD (2017) Education at a Glance 2017)

This graph shows where the educational expenditure comes from in each country. You can see the great variation in terms of expenditure sources for tertiary education among countries. Among the countries investigated, the average percentage of public expenditure on tertiary education is about 70 %, which means the national 1)_____ pay 70 % of the expenses spent on education in 2)_____, colleges and graduate schools. Finland provides its tertiary education almost 3)_____% based on public budget, whereas the Japanese government pays only 4)_____% of the expenses for tertiary education.

Task 9 ▸ Do research and discuss

1) What do you think about the expenditure on education in Japan?
2) How much do you spend on secondary or tertiary education?
3) Which do you prefer, the Finland-type distribution or the Japan-type distribution in terms of tertiary educational expenditure? Why do you think so?

5 | Reading graphs & charts 2

Enrollment and dropout rates   入学と退学の割合

Task 10 ▸ Fill in the blanks

01-39
039

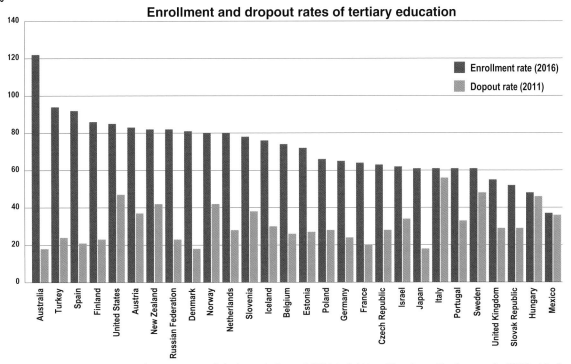

(Source: https://www.globalnote.jp/post-1465.html, https://honkawa2.sakura.ne.jp/3928a.html)

This graph shows the enrollment and dropout rates of tertiary education in each country. Australia has recorded a very high 1)_____ rate of about 120 %, which means not only people at or around the age of 18 but also a lot of older people enroll in universities and colleges for their further study. In some countries such as 2)_____, Australia and Denmark, the dropout rate is very low, whereas it is very high in 3)_____, Sweden, Hungary and the United States. In these countries it seems to be much more difficult for university students to 4)_____ than for Japanese students.

Task 11 ▸ Do research and discuss

1) What does studying at university mean to people in each country? Guess the differences.
2) Is there any relationship among the rate of public expenditure, entrance rate and dropout rate of tertiary education?

6 | Discussion & presentation

CD1-40
040

Jane and Toshi are talking about tertiary education. What do you think about the underlined parts especially? Do you agree with their opinions?

T: Hi, Jane. How was the sociology exam you took yesterday?

J: Hi, Toshi. I don't think I did very well.

T: Oh, really? Well, you can take the course again next year, even if you fail it this time. You're still in the third year of university, right?

J: You're right, but if I fail it again, then I may not be able to graduate next year. I don't want to stay in university for too long, because I have to pay tuition for semesters here in Japan, not for credits.

T: Mmm? What do you mean?

J: 1) <u>At some schools in the States, we pay tuition for the credits which we register for.</u> Suppose our university offers one credit for 200 dollars. Then, for example, if you register for 20 credits this semester, you pay 4,000 dollars. So it doesn't really matter how long you are in university, because the total number of credits is almost the same for everyone. But in Japan you have to pay for how long you belong to the university. The longer you belong to a university, the more you have to pay.

T: Ah, I see. The tuition payment system is different from country to country. 2) <u>I like the American way.</u>

J: Actually, in the States, there are many students who don't graduate from the university they first enter. Some of them just drop out, but many of them try to restart their study at another university by transferring the credits they earn at the first university.

T: You mean 3) <u>they don't hesitate to change universities?</u>

J: Yes, exactly. American students are very flexible about it.

Task 12 ▶ What do you think about tertiary education? How important is it for you? Is it worth paying a lot for tuition?

Unit 9 Appreciate the Arts

芸術を鑑賞する

1 Brainstorming

The arts include literature, music, the visual and graphic arts, the plastic arts, the decorative arts, the performing arts, and architecture. Look at the pictures. How do they make you feel? Which photo do you like best, and why?

• Warm up Talk to your classmate(s), and then listen to the explanation.

Task 1 ▸ Listen to the explanation and fill in the blanks

02-01
041

Art comes in many different forms across 1)_____ . When some people think about art, they think of painting or drawing. Others might think of music, dance, or 2)_____ . Art is a way to show creativity and imagination, and there are no 3)_____ to the ways that people can express themselves through art. Art is also 4)_____ . One person may find a painting or a song to be beautiful, but another person may not. In addition, art can evoke 5)_____ and emotions, and can be a powerful way to share a message or idea with others. Art is also a form of 6)_____ that can cross cultures. Even if you can't speak the language of a group, you can learn something about the group's 7)_____ , thoughts, or ideas through observing their art.

Task 2 ▸ Do shadowing

02-02
042

Task 3 ▸ Talk in pairs

1) What music inspires you most?
2) Do you like reading books? What books have you read?
3) Do you like dancing? Which type of dance do you like best?

2 | Word info 1

Task 4 Choose the most appropriate definition

1) **cultural goods**
   a) products that convey artistic, symbolic and aesthetic values
   b) products that are valuable because of their high cost, performance, and quality
   c) products that show the positive aspects of a culture

2) **abstract art**
   a) art that represents realistic concrete thoughts or ideas.
   b) art that uses colors, lines, and shapes without realistic visual depiction
   c) art that uses colors, lines, and shapes to create realistic images

3) **creativity**
   a) the ability to make things effectively, following the instructions of somebody
   b) the ability to make fascinating valuable products
   c) the ability to make new things or think of new ideas

4) **artisan**
   a) a person who is skilled at making things by hand
   b) a person who just knows how to make traditional things
   c) a person who majors in the history of making specific traditional goods

5) **renaissance**
   a) the new art that has changed the old traditional movement
   b) the great revival of art that began in Italy in the end of 14th century
   c) the old European art in the middle ages such as Christian paintings

Task 5 Discuss in pairs

1) What are some examples of cultural goods?
2) Is abstract art better or worse at communicating a thought or idea than lifelike art?

3 Word info 2

Task 6 Fill in the blanks with the words in the box. What do you think about free access to the arts?

> theaters   public viewing   entertainment   resources
> opportunity   donations   creative   funding   gallery

- England offers free entrance to its national art 1)_____ in London. Opening galleries to free 2)_____ makes art accessible to everyone, regardless of their income or socioeconomic status. However, this does not mean that everyone has access to art education. In fact, art programs are often the first to be cut from school 3)_____ when money for education runs short. For example, in a survey conducted by the BBC, it was found that 9 out of every 10 English schools surveyed had reduced lesson time, staff, or facilities in at least one 4)_____ arts subject. In addition, some classes are being cut completely, and according to the same survey, 1 in 10 schools are relying more on parents for 5)_____ toward maintaining art and music programs. Offering classes, such as drama, dance and music, is becoming difficult in England with limited financial 6)_____. This is true not only of England, but also of many countries around the world. Yet, if everyone is to have an equal 7)_____ to receive an arts education, then people must find creative solutions to this problem.

- The bar graph below shows how much England invested in the arts. At its peak in 2008/09, the inflation adjusted amount invested in the arts rose to £9.59 per person. In 2015/16 this had dropped to £5.87. This was a 39 % reduction. The types of funding used to create the 2007/08 baseline were: arts development and support, museums and galleries, and 8)_____ and public 9)_____.

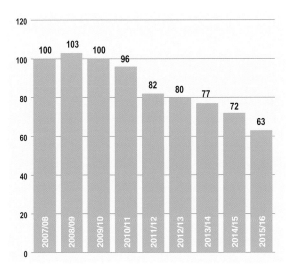

(Source: Forthearts.org.uk)

4 Reading graphs & charts 1

Creativity and life satisfaction 創作と生活満足度

CD2-03
↓ 043

Task 7 ▶ Fill in the blanks

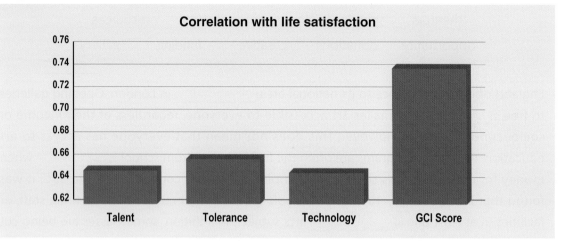

*The GCI is a measure for advanced economic growth and sustainable prosperity based on the 3Ts of economic development—talent, tolerance and technology.

(Source: Martin Prosperity Institute (2011))

The Global Creativity Index (GCI) measures and compares the 1)_____ of countries throughout the world. Each country is given a 2)_____ score. The higher the score, the more highly a country ranks in creativity. The above graph shows the relationship between life 3)_____ in a country and factors, such as talent, 4)_____, technology, and the GCI score. We can see from the graph that the GCI score is most related with life satisfaction. This means that if a country has a 5)_____ GCI score, then its population is more likely to have high 6)_____ satisfaction.

Task 8 ▶ Do research and discuss

1) Which has a bigger impact on life satisfaction, tolerance or talent?
2) Why do you think creativity is so closely related with life satisfaction?
3) Do you think it's possible to measure a country's creativity accurately?

5 Reading graphs & charts 2

Exports of cultural goods 文化財の輸出

Task 9 ▸ Fill in the blanks

02-04
044

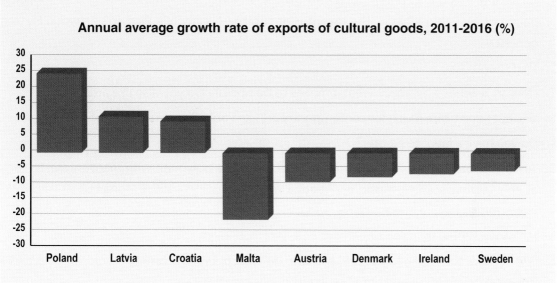

Annual average growth rate of exports of cultural goods, 2011-2016 (%)

(Source: Eurostat)

The graph above shows the annual average growth rate of 1)_____ of cultural goods
in eight countries around the world. According to the graph, 2)_____ had the biggest
increase by 24 % in exporting 3)_____ between the years 2011 to 2016, while Malta
had the biggest decrease by -21%. According to Eurostat, the overall 4)_____ in exporting
of cultural goods in Malta and Denmark was triggered by the fall in the 5)_____ of jewelry
Meanwhile, the increase in exports in Poland was caused by the increase of audio-visual and
6)_____ media, such as films and books.

Task 10 ▸ Do research and discuss

1) Do you think the global trade of cultural goods can affect rural artisans?
2) Do you expect that Japan will import more cultural goods over the next 5 years? Why or
   why not?

CD2-05
⬇ 045

Sakura and Toshi are talking about creativity and their favorite artists. What do you think about the underlined parts especially? Do you agree with their opinions?

T: Hi, Sakura. I visited a contemporary art gallery, which has a temporary exhibition of some paintings by Pablo Picasso, the inventor of cubism. I really like Picasso's artwork. He is a genius!

S: That sounds fun.

T: I feel art teaches a lot about what it means to be human. Do you also like art?

S: Yes, but I don't care much for contemporary art like Pablo Picasso's paintings.

T: Do you have a favorite painter?

S: Yes, my favorite painter is Leonardo da Vinci. He was a polymath with many interests, such as engineering, science, music, and math. He was the painter of the Mona Lisa. 1) <u>The world needs more creative minds like his.</u>

T: I think we should focus on one thing.

S: I don't think so. It's inspiring that Leonardo da Vinci pursued a variety of interests. He had a powerful imagination and didn't set limits on his creativity.

T: He must have been very talented.

S: 2) <u>I believe anyone can be creative.</u>

T: That might be so, but not everyone has the same opportunity to be creative. The best way to develop creativity is by increasing funding of art education.

S: I disagree. 3) <u>I think everybody should have an equal opportunity to study art, but school is not the only place where we can learn about the arts.</u> For example, some museums provide free public access, and we can also check out resources from the library.

T: We should help people understand the impact of art on the community, personal development, and culture. The world needs young people who can become the next Pablo Picasso or Leonardo da Vinci.

Task 11 ▶ What do you think about the importance of creativity and art?

Unit 10

See the Potential of Artificial Intelligence (AI)

AI の発展可能性を見る

1 Brainstorming

Look at the picture. It seems a vehicle is working in the desert. It has some arms and tires. What is it doing there? And what do you think it is?

©NASA/JPL/Cornell University

Warm up Talk to your classmate(s), and then listen to the explanation.

Task 1 Listen to the explanation and fill in the blanks

02-06
046

For many years, science and technology experts have studied how to make 1)_____ that can allow robots to interact naturally with humans. More and more robots have 2)_____ features and body structures, which can help create the illusion of life. Scientists have recently focused on producing a new aspect of humanity in robots: 3)_____. Culture can be defined as the ideas, customs, and behaviors of a group of people or society. At MIT's Computer Science and Artificial Intelligence Laboratory (CSAIL), a roboticist and computer scientist 4)_____ a system that allows robots to learn from human programming, and 5)_____. If robots can pass on knowledge through social learning, then they can also share and 6)_____ on culture. Some see this as a step toward creating robots that can aid intercultural collaboration.

Task 2 Do shadowing

02-07
047

Task 3 Talk in pairs

1) If you could invent a robot, what type of robot would you create?
2) Do you believe a robot can acquire the same level of intelligence as a human?
3) How can AI encourage intercultural collaboration?

67

Task 4 Match the definition with the words related to AI

1) Definition: a field of computer science devoted to making computers perform tasks in ways that would normally require human intelligence
   a) real intelligence
   b) artificial reasoning
   c) artificial intelligence

2) Definition: any type of computer software that people can modify and share
   a) open origin software
   b) open source software
   c) closed source software

3) Definition: the learning process of using artificial intelligence to make it possible for a machine to learn from and improve its performance
   a) machine learning
   b) appliance learning
   c) artificial learning

4) Definition: a device which detects or measures physical properties of the world, such as light, heat and moisture
   a) a sensor
   b) a meter
   c) a measure

5) Definition: knowledge about the world that humans are expected to know
   a) common sense knowledge
   b) common nonsense knowledge
   c) uncommon sense knowledge

Task 5 Talk in pairs

1) Are you interested in AI?
2) Do you believe AI can become a threat to humans? Why or why not?

3 Word info 2

Task 6 Fill in the blanks with the words in the box. What do you think about AI technology?

> source code   features   customize   virtual   DNA
>
> programmers   partnership   open source

During the early years of computers, people who wanted to create documents or design 1)_____ art projects often chose to buy expensive software such as Microsoft, Apple, or Adobe products. However, with progress in 2)_____ software, computer users can use publicly accessible programs. A source code is like the 3)_____ of a software program, which tells it how to work. Because the 4)_____ of open source software is publically viewable, those with programming abilities can 5)_____ the coding of open source software to change how the program works, fix errors, or add new 6)_____. This even makes it possible for 7)_____ to translate software into new languages. The existence of open source software also gives people the ability to share knowledge about AI. For example, recent technology giants, such as Microsoft, Google and Facebook, have decided to share the source code of their systems, to allow for more global 8)_____ in the way that technology is developed and used.

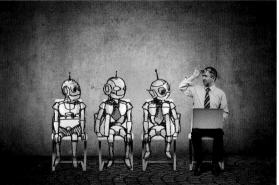

4 Reading graphs & charts 1

Robotic operating systems (ROS) ロボットオペレーティングシステム (ROS)

Task 7 Fill in the blanks

CD2-08
⬇ 048

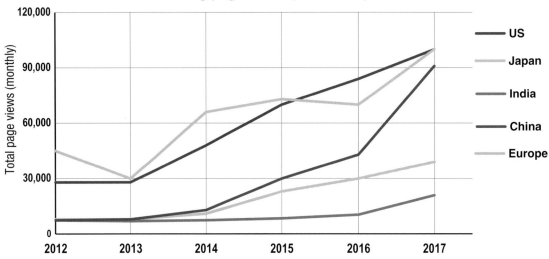

ROS. org page views (2012-2017)

(Source: ROS metrics report)

ROS stands for "Robotic Operating System." It is the name of an online resource of downloadable open source software for robotics. This graph is from *The 2018 AI Index report*. It shows the areas of the world that have the greatest number of 1)_____ of the ROS website between the years 2)_____ and 2017. According to the graph, the 3)_____ and Europe had the greatest number of page views in 2017. In addition, China has showed a recent spike in views. For example, the number of page views in 2017 was about 4)_____ times the number of views in 2012. The ROS site reports that the 5)_____ in web traffic from China is organic, meaning that ROS did not increase its marketing toward Chinese readers, but instead, China showed an increased interest in 6)_____ without any influence from the website.

Task 8 Do research and discuss

1) Which country has shown a more rapid increase in ROS page views: India or the US?
2) Why do you think Europe's ROS page views decreased from 2015 to 2016?
3) Do you believe that all software should be open source? Why or why not?

5 | Reading graphs & charts 2

The hot topics in AI research   AI 研究の話題

 Task 9 ▸ Fill in the blanks

D2-09
049

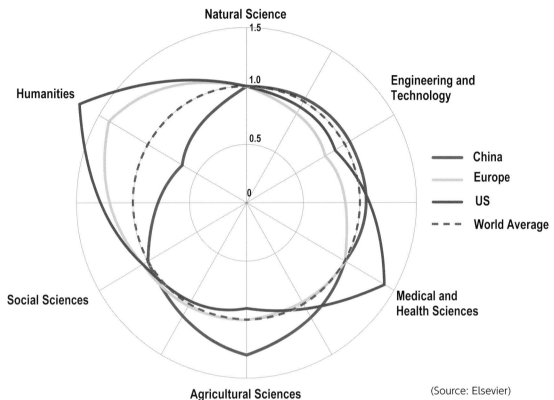

(Source: Elsevier)

AI is used for many purposes, such as to improve medicine and to better harvest crops. Since every country has different problems and economic needs, each country focuses its research efforts on different areas. For example, in *The 2018 AI Index report*, a study was conducted on the subject of AI papers compiled in 1)_____, 2)_____, and 3)_____. According to the report, AI papers in China focused more on the sectors of 4)_____, natural sciences and 5)_____, while papers in the US and Europe focused more on 6)_____. China is a major food producer. This suggests that the country focuses on agricultural sciences, partly because it wants to create 7)_____ technology to help improve its food industry.

Task 10 ▸ Do research and discuss

1) Which areas of AI research did Europe focus most on in 2017?
2) Which areas of study (engineering, natural sciences, etc.) would most benefit from developments in AI? Why do you think so?

6 Discussion & presentation

CD2-10
↓ 050

Jane and Xiaoxue are talking about AI and ethics. What do you think about the underlined parts especially? Do you agree with their opinions?

X: Hello, Jane. Nice to see you. Are you on your way home?

J: Hi, Xiaoxue. Yeah, good to see you. I just returned from giving a presentation at an international science conference.

X: That's great! What did you talk about at the conference?

J: I discussed why 1) <u>it is important that scientists observe a code of ethics when manufacturing machines with AI.</u>

X: That sounds interesting but difficult. One of the biggest worries people have may be that 2) <u>robots will take people's jobs.</u>

J: That's it. Unemployment is a concern for some, but there are other ethical problems, too. For example, systems such as AI sensors can make mistakes in ways that humans can't, and depending on the way that machines are programmed, they might show bias rather than fair judgement. Robots can also be a security risk.

X: I see. That's a lot to consider. Do you still believe that robots can be helpful?

J: Absolutely! I believe that 3) <u>AI is a necessary part of world progress.</u> Thanks to advancements in AI, people can complete difficult tasks with ease and better communicate with people in different countries.

X: I hope that people can lead easier lives because of assistance from robots. However, what I want most is a robot that can teach me to speak a new language well!

Task 11 What do you think about artificial intelligence and its relation to ethics?

Unit 11

Change Your Attitude toward Gender Roles

男女の役割の考え方を変える

1 Brainstorming

Saudi Arabia is finally set to allow women to drive cars. It might be the last country in the world to do so. You see a woman driving a car in this picture. Do you think she looks happy?

Warm up Talk to your classmate(s), and then listen to the news.

D2-11
051

Task 1 Listen to the news and fill in the blanks

June 24, 2018 was a great day for women in Saudi Arabia. On that day, some Saudi Arabian 1)_____ drove by themselves in public for the first time. Saudi Arabia, the 2)_____ country in the Middle East, is an absolute monarchy, which follows a conservative Muslim sect called Wahhabism. According to its 3)_____, women were not allowed to go out without a 4)_____ guardian. That is why driver's licenses had not been given to women, because the guardian is supposed to be able to 5)_____. In 2017, Crown Prince Mohammed bin Salman issued a decree that 6)_____ driving should be allowed as part of the program for modernization. It is reported that about 7)_____ women were given driver's licenses in the first week of the removal of the 8)_____ in June 2018. However, there are still some restrictions related to women's rights in Saudi Arabia. For example, women need their male guardians to marry and divorce, get a job, and open a bank 9)_____ . Also, girls' sports activities are prohibited in public schools.

D2-12
052

Task 2 Do shadowing

Task 3 Talk in pairs

1) Who often drives in your family?
2) Is there any difference between female drivers and male drivers?
3) Is there anything that men often do, but women seldom do?

2 Word info 1

Task 4 Look at the box and the word list below. You can see the categories 'Male/men' on the left and 'Female/women' on the right of the box and a number of human activities in the word list. As in the example below, write each activity in the box to show which gender role you think should be associated with it.

Male/men ←———————————————→ **Female/women**

e.g. practicing sumo   e.g. working as a nurse

Word list

driving   smoking   fishing   farming   hunting   doing laundry
wearing a skirt   wearing a necktie   wearing a pair of jeans
working as a doctor   working as a nurse   working as a police officer
working as a firefighter   working as a bus driver   working as a taxi driver
teaching at an elementary school   teaching at a high school
playing football   playing baseball   playing rugby   practicing sumo

Task 5 Are there any things that are done only by men or women?

Task 6 Discuss in pairs

1) Look at the picture on the previous page. What is the woman wearing? Why is she wearing it?

2) Look at the people in the picture on the top of this page. They are wearing skirts. Are they male or female? What do you think about this?

3   Word info 2

Task 7   Quiz

Q1 Household chores are tasks done regularly at home such as washing, cleaning, and ironing. What does the phrase "household chores" mean to you?

a) tasks that children should do
b) tasks that husbands or fathers should do
c) tasks that wives or mothers should do
d) tasks that every family member should do

Q2 The national assembly is a meeting or gathering that is composed of the representatives of a nation. What does the phrase "representatives of the national assembly" mean to you?

a) It's a role for men.
b) The number of male and female representatives should be the same.
c) There should be both male and female representatives, but the ratio of men versus women doesn't matter.
d) There should be more women than men who carry out the job.

©mizuola/iStockphoto.com

Q3 Which of the following best describes 'multitasking'?

a) Toru has several official positions such as teacher at a school and chair of the PTA. He is a committee member on the city's globalization and tourism.
b) Junko is good at doing several things at the same time. For example, she can read a book, take care of her baby daughter, and do the laundry, all while preparing dinner.
c) Kimiko has several part-time jobs. She works at a supermarket on Monday and Friday, and at a family restaurant on Tuesday and Thursday.
d) Masa changes his job frequently. He used to be a mail carrier for two years, became a taxi driver after that and he became a cook one year later. Now he enjoys working as a teacher at a cram school.

4 Reading graphs & charts 1

Husbands and household chores 夫と家事

 Task 8 Fill in the blanks

CD2-13
↓ 053

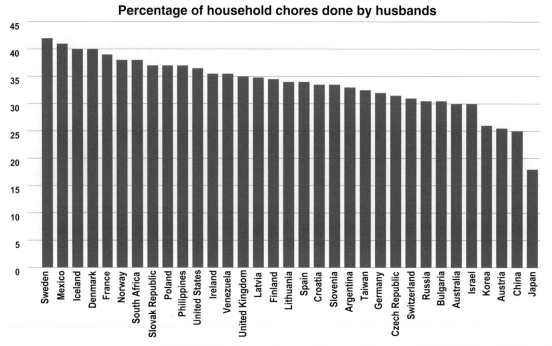

Percentage of household chores done by husbands

(Source: https://www.newsweekjapan.jp/stories/world/2016/03/post-4607.php)

This graph shows what percentage of household chores husbands do in each country. Generally speaking, the husbands in 1)_____ European countries do a lot of household chores: 42.7 % in Sweden, 40.1 % in Denmark, and 38.0 % in Norway. In most countries investigated, more than 30 % of household chores are taken over by husbands; however, the percentage is relatively 2)_____ in Asian countries such as Korea and Japan. In particular, the husbands in 3)_____ do the least household chores at home: they take over only 18.3 % of them.

Task 9 Do research and discuss

1) Do you agree with household chores done by men?
2) Do you feel that there are gender differences in household chores?
3) Do your parents work? Who does household chores in your family? How about your friends' families?

5 Reading graphs & charts 2

Female representatives in national assemblies 国会における女性代表

Task 10   Fill in the blanks

CD2-14
054

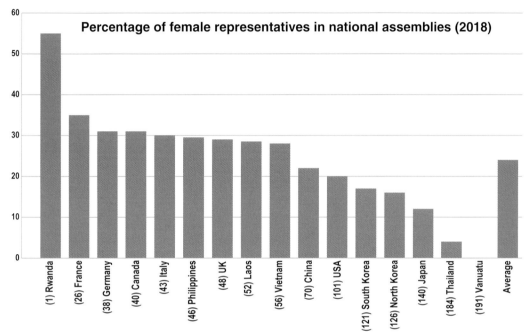

(Source: https://www.globalnote.jp/post-3877.html)

This graph shows the percentage of female representatives in the national assemblies in some countries. Among the 193 countries and areas investigated, 1)_____ has the highest percentage (55.7 %), while the lowest are Vanuatu, Micronesia and Papua New Guinea (0 %). The average is 23.4 %. In Asian countries, 2)_____, Laos and Vietnam have relatively higher percentages (above 25 %), whereas there are less than 10 % of female representatives in national assemblies in 3)_____. The percentage of Japan is 13.7 %, which is ranked as the 4)_____th of all the 193 countries investigated.

Task 11   Do research and discuss

1) Is there any tendency of the percentage of female representatives in different areas (Europe, America, Asia, Africa, etc.)?

2) What do you think about the percentage in Japan? Do you think it should be higher? Why or why not?

6 Discussion & presentation

CD2-15
↓ 055

Sakura and Paul are talking about working mothers. What do you think about the underlined parts especially? Do you agree with their opinions?

S: Hi, Paul. Does your mother work?

P: Yes, my mother works at a bank. But, why do you ask, Sakura?

S: My mother is a housewife now, and she is thinking of taking a job. But my father is against the idea. He 1) <u>probably just wants her to stay at home and do household chores.</u>

P: Oh, really? My mother works full time, but my father doesn't seem to have any complaints about it.

S: Does your father do household chores?

P: Yes, sure. Not so much as my mother does, though.

S: My father doesn't do any household chores at home. He wants her to do all the chores by staying at home.

P: Ha-ha. It seems that your father is a traditional Japanese man. 2) <u>I recommend he take over some fixed tiny chores first, like cleaning the bathroom or doing the laundry.</u> That's what my father does.

S: I'll persuade my father to try it, but it's so hard.

P: Personally, I think 3) <u>women should work more outside of the home because they have better working skills than men do,</u> like networking skills, speech skills, tolerance and multitasking skills. My mother is even thinking of running for the role of a representative of the prefectural assembly.

S: Wow, that's great! But there are not many female representatives in the assembly, right?

P: Certainly not. There are only 2 women out of 75 people, which means about 2.7 %.

S: That's too low.

Task 12 What do you think about gender roles in your family, local community, school and country? What would happen if the national assembly had more female representatives in Japan?

Unit 12

Live Well in a Cashless Society

キャッシュレス社会をうまく生きる

1 Brainstorming

Look at these pictures. Do you know the differences between these cards? They look similar, but are very different! If you know how they are different, you can buy things more easily. Let's think about cashless society.

Warm up Talk to your classmate(s), and then listen to the news.

Task 1 Listen to the news and fill in the blanks

02-16
056

There are so many ways of making payments today. In the past we had to have a 1)_____ for shopping, but that is not the case now. As long as we have these cards, we don't have to carry a heavy wallet. Among them, the 2)_____ cards can be started most easily. For example, PASMO, one of the most famous prepaid cards in Japan, can be bought at the vending 3)_____ in almost every train station. There is no need to report your private information to companies. It is very convenient because you can use this card for 4)_____ train tickets and for shopping in almost every 5)_____ store in Japan. But if you use another card, you even don't have to take time to recharge: it's a 6)_____ card. When you buy things with the card, the payment will be automatically charged to your bank 7)_____ next month of the shopping, so you don't have to recharge the card. Thanks to these cards, our society is now becoming a cashless 8)_____.

Task 2 Do shadowing

02-17
057

Task 3 Talk in pairs

1) Have you ever used a credit card? If not, do you want to have your own credit card?
2) Are you afraid of a cashless society? What do you think about this?
3) What is the difference between a prepaid card and a debit card? Which do you like?

2 Word info 1

Task 4 Fill in the blanks with the words in the box.

> Cash   Euro   Currency   E-money   Virtual currency

a) (   ) refers to any type of money such as dollars or yen.

b) (   ) refers to money in the physical form of coins and bills.

c) (   ) is digital money that can be used among the members of the currency's virtual community.

d) (   ) is a monetary unit used in the European union.

e) (   ) is a type of money stored electronically on devices such as computers or plastic cards.

Task 5 Check the meanings of the highlighted words and look them up in the English–English dictionary.

a) In Canada, many people use **e-money**. The percentage of e-money payments is about 57 % of all payments in the country. One of the reasons for this high percentage is that it is difficult to set up **ATMs** in such a large country as Canada. People can **withdraw** cash from their **bank accounts** through ATM. Because of the difficulty in using cash, the country is now becoming more like a **cashless** society.

b) People in Germany don't seem to use **credit cards** often. The average number of credit card ownership **per capita** is less than 0.1. The number is quite low compared with the number of the US, which is about 3.0. The country is also reluctant to accept **cryptocurrency**, saying that type of currency could lead to **economic crisis** in the future.

c) Japan seems to be willing to realize a cashless society. In 2014 the country aimed at increasing the percentage of **cashless** payments by 2020. Also, **cryptocurrency** such as **Bitcoin** is more and more popular in the country. However, Japan is an **aging society**, so there are many old people more willing to use cash.

Task 6 Discuss in pairs

What do you think about the current cashless situations in Canada, Germany and Japan? Which country is the most cashless society? Do you like such a cashless society?

3 Word info 2

Task 7 Fill in the blanks with the words in the box. Which topic is interesting to you? Why do you think so?

> leaked   cashless society   cashless payment   profits
>
> smartphone   big data   bank account

- There are so many ways of 1)_____. Some years ago cash and debit cards were often used for making payments, but now the trend is changing rapidly mainly because of the development of ICT. If you have a credit card, you can use a 2)_____ as a credit card by entering the payment information. Instead of having a heavy wallet, you can enjoy shopping just by using your smartphone.
- In some countries, the technology is more advanced. In Sweden, you don't even have to have a credit card account. If you just have a 3)_____ and a mobile phone number, you can shop with your smartphone thanks to the application that the Swedish banks made.
- In a 4)_____, almost all the data of customers' shopping can be stored and traced back easily and quickly, because all the shopping records are digitized. That means companies can get 5)_____ for business. With the data, they can make decisions more effectively to get more 6)_____. For example, if a company can precisely expect with the data how many goods will be sold in a specific month, they can decide effectively the amount of goods they will produce. This can enhance their earnings, because they can avoid overproduction.
- If some companies successfully collect big precise data, they can even sell the data to other companies. However, there is also a risk of possessing big data. If attacked by a hacker, the data can be 7)_____ and the company can lose its fame and may have to compensate for damages by spending a lot of money.

4 Reading graphs & charts 1

Cryptocurrency 暗号通貨

Task 8 Fill in the blanks

CD2-18
↓ 058

Bitcoin price index from August 2017 to August 2019 (US dollars)

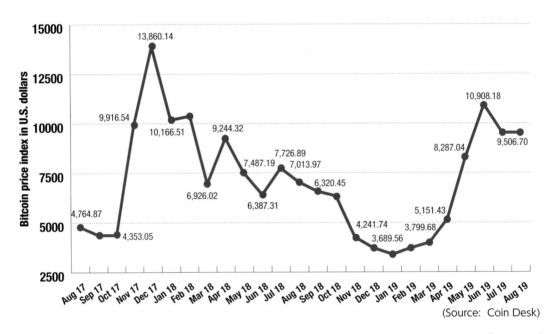

(Source: Coin Desk)

This graph shows how many 1)_____ were equal to one Bitcoin in a specific period from August 2017 to August 2)_____. Bitcoin is the first cryptocurrency. It is the most famous digital 3)_____, but it seems to be still unstable. Let's check the price behavior of Bitcoin for the 4)_____ years. According to the graph, the price of one Bitcoin was first 5)_____ than 5,000 dollars, but the price rapidly rose to 13,860 dollars in 6)_____ 2017. After that, the price in March 2018 saw a big 7)_____ to 6,926 dollars. In January 2019, the price bottomed out at less than 3,500 dollars, but it rose up again. Accordingly, Bitcoin is not stable.

Task 9 Do research and discuss

1) What is the difference between cryptocurrency and e-money?
2) What is the merit of using Bitcoin?
3) Do you want to have Bitcoins?

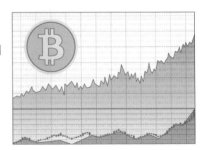

5 Reading graphs & charts 2

Currency exchange 為替

Task 10 Fill in the blanks

02-19
059

Euro (EUR) to US dollar (USD) annual average exchange rate from 1999 to 2018

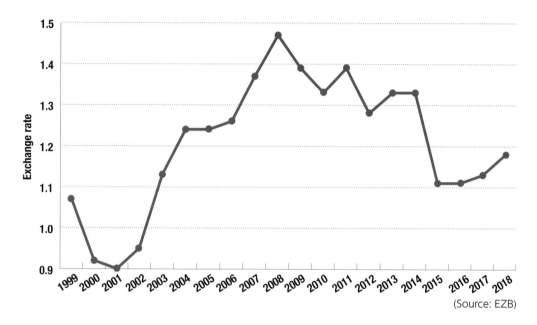

(Source: EZB)

This graph shows how many dollars were equal to one Euro during a specific period. The price started with about 1.1 dollars, but it gradually dropped. After 1)_____ the price started to go up, and in 2)_____ the price went up to the highest of about 3)_____ . But after that, the price gradually started to decrease to about 1.3 dollars in 4)_____ and further to less than 1.2 dollars in 5)_____ . As the graph shows, the price was not steady, especially from 2000 to 2010. In that sense, the Euro might not have been a reliable currency during those periods.

Task 11 Do research and discuss

1) How many dollars are equal to one euro now?
2) How many yen are equal to one euro now?
3) Which currency do you think is most reliable?

6 Discussion & presentation

CD2-20
060

Xiaoxue and Toshi are talking about cashless society. What do you think about the underlined parts especially? Do you agree with their opinions?

T: Hi, Xiaoxue. I'm so excited! I'm going to buy a smartphone to pay for things.

X: Oh, really? But you shouldn't forget that there are risks to making cashless payments.

T: You are right. If I lose my smartphone, someone will buy things with it. But, we can experience the same problems from having a wallet. If we lose our wallets, someone could use the money inside.

X: There's more to it than that. 1) Cashless payments can confuse our sense of money.

T: I know what you mean. I disagree with having a completely cashless society.

X: That might be true. I don't mean a cashless society is always bad. I know it has pros and cons. One of the advantages is that the government can collect taxes easily. Companies can also collect a lot of customer data easily.

T: Exactly. However, collecting data can actually cause problems. If data collectors are attacked by hackers, their information can be stolen. 2) This is a serious problem, because it may include important information such as its PIN number.

X: Oh, that's so scary. I'm going to use a debit card when I travel to other countries. In China, fake cash caused a very big social issue, and it was often difficult to distinguish whether cash was genuine or not. That's one of the reasons why part of China is now nearly a cashless society.

T: Oh, even using cash can be risky. 3) Perhaps we may need to return to a barter society.

Task 12 ▸ What do you think about cashless society?

Pray for No More Wars and Just Peace

戦争がなく平和をただ祈る

1 Brainstorming

Look at these pictures. One is a photo of Mahatma Gandhi, the father of India. The other shows the flag of Switzerland. It might be difficult to find something in common, but both images remind us of world peace. Let's think about it — what can you do to make the world more peaceful?

Warm up Talk to your classmate(s), and then listen to the explanation.

Task 1 Listen to the explanation and fill in the blanks

"If we want to reach real peace in this world, we should start 1)_____ children." "In a gentle way, we can shake the world." These are quotes from Mahatma Gandhi. Since 1858 India had been governed by 2)_____ for more than 80 years. India wanted to be independent from England, so a lot of violent conflicts occurred. But from 3)_____, when Gandhi started to lead the movement, many people used no 4)_____ to protest their ideas. Gandhi repeatedly said that having love and compassion for others can be a much 5)_____ protest than using violence to them. Finally, in 1947 India became independent from England, but just one year after that Gandhi was 6)_____. Ironically, violence ended his life. He refused using violence for peace, but one peaceful country took a 7)_____ way. Switzerland wasn't involved with any conflicts even in the period of World War II. That was because the country was recognized as a neutral country. It means that Switzerland does not join any battles or wars between nations. In order to obtain this position, Switzerland has a military draft 8)_____.

Task 2 Do shadowing

Task 3 Talk in pairs

1) Have you ever used violence to protest?
2) Do you agree violence is necessary to make a peaceful community?
3) Why did Switzerland choose to be neutral in the world?

2 Word info 1

Task 4 Quiz

Q1 Fill in the blanks with the words in the box.

| conflict   alliance   neutrality |

a) If two groups are in (   ), they support each other.
b) If two groups are in (   ), they battle against each other.
c) If two groups are in (   ), they don't interfere with each other.

Q2 Which best describes the words: 1) data leakage, 2) cyber war, and 3) hacking?

a) One day a Japanese company falsely posted its customers' privacy onto the Internet. The cause of this incident was that one of its employees used a computer which was infected with computer viruses. The employee said he didn't know when the computer got infected, though he got anonymous email some days before the leakage. The company's supervisors concluded that the e-mail contained the viruses inside, but couldn't identify who sent the e-mail.

b) One day a nation's website was attacked by someone. The website was widely accessed, causing the nation's server to stop and the website couldn't be browsed for a while. A careful inspection concluded that the access was from its neighboring country. Some days before the attack those two countries had had a conflict over trading policy. They also thought that the attack was the protest from the country saying that the policy should be changed.

c) One day a public employee lost his flash drive. It had a lot of important information about the nation's education policy, but he didn't report to his boss that he had lost the drive. After a while all the important information was uploaded onto the Internet by someone who accidentally picked up the flash drive. Because of this incident, the nation lost the trust of its people.

Task 5 Discuss in pairs

1) Do you know about cyber security? How should you be careful about data leakage and hacking?

2) Are you afraid of a cyber war? What do you think about the cases described above?

3 Word info 2

Task 6 Fill in the blanks with the words in the box. And discuss the two topics: using guns and nuclear power.

> electricity   violence   nuclear warheads   firearms
>
> self-defense   renewable energy   nuclear power

• Should 1)_____ be allowed to use to protect ourselves? Using guns or rifles for 2)_____ is not so common in Japan, but it is a more familiar practice in the US and Switzerland, as the graph shows. But more or less we use 3)_____ when we protect ourselves. For example, if you confronted by a suspicious man holding a knife, would you prepare yourself for the possibility of a fight? What is the difference between hitting someone and using a gun to protect yourself?

• Now we need more eco-friendly ways of making electricity. Although 4)_____ resources are sustainable, they can't make a lot of electricity in a short period. However, using 5)_____, we can generate tons of energy very quickly without emitting nearly any CO_2 into the atmosphere. More and more countries are becoming interested in this way of generating 6)_____ .

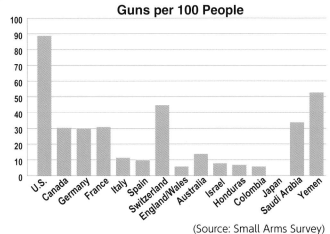

(Source: Small Arms Survey)

• Russia has tried to meet this demand to make profits. In fact, in April 2018 it started to build the first nuclear power plant in Turkey. However, we need to be careful about this trend. If one country has nuclear technology, that means that the country can also make dangerous weapons such as 7)_____ by itself.

Gun owning 銃所有

CD2-23
↓ 063

Task 7 ▶ Fill in the blanks

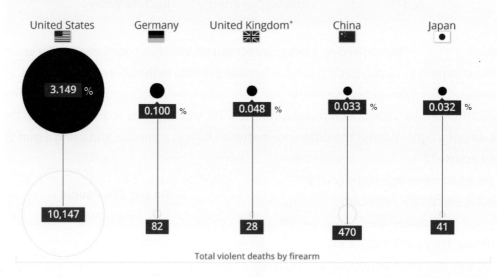

Firearm Deaths in the World's Largest Economies
Violent deaths involving a firearm per 100,000 population in 2016

United States	Germany	United Kingdom*	China	Japan
3.149 %	0.100 %	0.048 %	0.033 %	0.032 %
10,147	82	28	470	41

Total violent deaths by firearm

* England and Wales
@StatistaCharts Source: Small Arms Survey

statista

This figure shows the percentage of firearm deaths per 100,000 population in five countries. 1)_____ has the highest percentage, 3.149 %. All of the other countries have a very low percentage, less than 2)_____ %. However, the number of the total violent deaths by 3)_____ in China is larger than the UK, Germany, and Japan. This is because China has a lot more 4)_____ than the other three countries. Here we should focus on the percentage of firearm death in 5)_____ , where as many as 5.4 million guns are legally owned by its people. It is just 0.1 %. This is because the country has a very strict law 6)_____ guns. The strong restriction was made after the country experienced a case of mass 7)_____ or gun violence.

Task 8 ▶ Do research and discuss

1) Do you agree that people in Japan should be allowed to own a gun without having a license?
2) Some people in the United States think that they need to own guns to protect themselves. Do you think they should stop owning guns? Why or why not?

5 | **Reading graphs & charts 2**

Nuclear warheads 核弾頭

Task 9 ▶ Fill in the blanks

02-24
↓ 064

The countries with the biggest nuclear arsenals
Number of nuclear warheads in countries worldwide in 2015

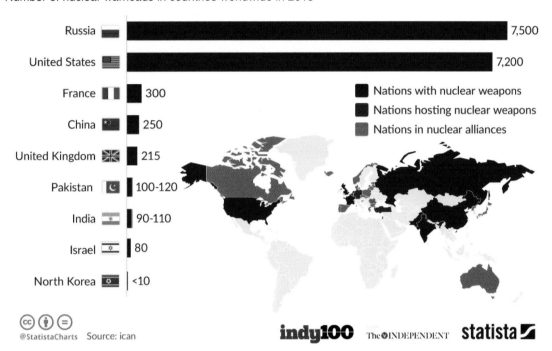

@StatistaCharts   Source: ican

This figure shows the number of nuclear warheads each country has. In other words, the number shows roughly how many times each country can make nuclear explosions by using 1)_____ . Russia has the most nuclear warheads, followed by 2)_____ in second place. The two countries have more than 3)_____% of all the nuclear warheads on the Earth. France comes in third place. The country is also famous for making a lot of 4)_____ with nuclear power plants. Japan is in 5)_____ alliances, which means the country is protected by nations with nuclear 6)_____.

Task 10 ▶ Do research and discuss

1) Do you agree that developed countries should own nuclear weapons to protect themselves?
2) Should Japan be in nuclear alliances?
3) What do you think about nuclear power?

6 Discussion & presentation

Paul and Toshi are talking about war and peace. What do you think about the underlined parts especially? Do you agree with their opinions?

T: I'm studying about the Israeli-Palestinian conflict in my social studies class. I'm so shocked that the conflict started because the British government told lies to both Jews and Arabs.

P: Well, that's not the only reason for the conflict. I believe that 1) we can stop having such problems if we can mutually understand and respect the differences between people groups.

T: Exactly. To be honest, I think any kind of differences can cause conflicts.

P: Knowing each other well is very important for world peace. I think the key to success is education.

T: Absolutely. It's important to respect different cultures.

P: Yes, but wars or conflicts are not always caused by the differences. I hope they are decreasing.

T: That's true, but some people say that such traditional wars will decrease because of a new type of war. It's a cyber war. However it will not be a solution. 2) Pursuing "negative peace" never leads to a peaceful world.

P: What do you mean by "negative peace"?

T: "Negative peace" refers to the condition that we have no conflicts, so pursuing "negative peace" means that we try to stop conflicts and wars to ensure that society has no violence in it.

P: Do you mean we need to make our attitude more "positive"?

T: Yeah, but sometimes I wonder if this idea is too idealistic.

P: Well, it is a bit idealistic, though I like the idea. 3) We should start by being kind to our neighbors to make a better society.

T: Ah, that sounds interesting. Small things add up to make a great difference. Our small kindness could also add up to creating world peace.

Task 11 ▶ What do you think about war and peace?

Unit 14 Address Immigration Issues

移民問題に取り組む

1 Brainstorming

Look at this poster. Can you read the language? It's not English. —it's French. The title says "La Cour de Babel." It is the title of a film, and it is a film made in France. The title means "School of Babel" in English. The film shows a school in France. What do you think the story is about?

Warm up Talk to your classmate(s), and then listen to the synopsis.

Task 1 Listen to the synopsis and fill in the blanks

02-26
066

A French film, La Cour de Babel, which means School of Babel in English, follows a 1)_____ in a Paris classroom for children who have recently immigrated to France. It shows the 2)_____ of children who have come to France from Mauritania, Serbia, Venezuela, Rumania, Senegal, Libya, Ireland, Brazil, and China. You can see how diverse and complex their 3)_____ is, wrestling with a new language and a new 4)_____. The film builds to a powerful climax when it comes time for them to say goodbye to each other and their 5)_____. This film talks about their shared experiences in cultural defferences, and is an inspiring source of 6)_____ for France and the world.

Task 2 Do shadowing

02-27
067

Task 3 Talk in pairs

1) Do you want to see this film?
2) What do you expect the story is about?
3) Do you have any friends from other countries?
4) What do you think about immigrants?

91

Q1 What do these words mean?

1) **immigrant**
   a) a person that has not yet arrived
   b) a person who flees to a country for safety in a time of war or conflict
   c) a person who goes to another country usually for permanent residence

2) **refugee**
   a) a person that has just arrived
   b) a person who flees to another country for safety in a time of war or conflict
   c) a person who goes to a peaceful country usually for permanent residence

3) **newcomer**
   a) a person that has recently arrived
   b) a person who flees to a foreign country for safety in a time of war or conflict
   c) a person who lives in another country, usually for permanent residence

Q2 Is the following person an immigrant, a refugee, a newcomer or something else?

 He was born in Syria. One day he had to escape from the country with his family due to a terrible civil war. Luckily he came to Japan two years ago, but couldn't go back to Syria.

 She was born in China. One day she decided to do volunteer work in a developing country. She worked there for one year and tried to help many poor people in the country. She stayed at a building made by the UN.

 He was born in America. One day he found himself quite interested in Japanese culture, so he decided to study Japanese culture as a university student in Japan. He was in the country for two years, and stayed at his Japanese friend Ken's house.

 She was born in Japan. She started to work as a professional table tennis player in Japan three years ago. One day she decided to play table tennis in Germany, so she moved to the country. Since she liked the country very much, she obtained the German nationality. She never came back to Japan.

In your town, do you see immigrants or refugees? If yes, please share your experiences. If no, think about why you don't see immigrants or refugees in your area of living.

3 ▸ Word info 2

Task 6 ▸ Quiz

Q1 What does terrorism mean to you? Why do you think so?

a) attacking other people without specific reasons

b) placing a bomb in a very popular shopping mall and making fun of police officers

c) using violence to protest something

d) sending a bunch of email to the government to claim something

Q2 What does religion mean to you? Why do you think so?

a) a strong sense of loving somebody

b) a belief in and worship of God or gods

c) a hope that your favorite baseball team will win a championship

d) a belief that there are aliens in space

Q3 What does a global company mean to you? Which case best suits your understanding?

a) Geegle is a company that makes EV cars in China. The company doesn't export the cars to other countries, but it is planning to sell the cars in other countries in the near future. Geegle has many employees, who are all Chinese.

b) Tsuyota is a company that makes airplanes in America. Its planes are used in many countries, but its factories are only in America. Tsuyota has many employees who are from many different countries.

c) Footbook is a company that makes fascinating amusement parks in many countries. It originally started its business in Japan, but as its business got bigger, the company made a lot of branches in other countries. Now its employees are from many countries, but it is criticized these days because it never employs African Americans.

4 Reading graphs & charts 1

Immigration in Germany ドイツの移民

CD2-28
⬇ 068

Task 7 ▶ Fill in the blanks

The long history of immigration in Germany
Arrivals in Germany since 1950

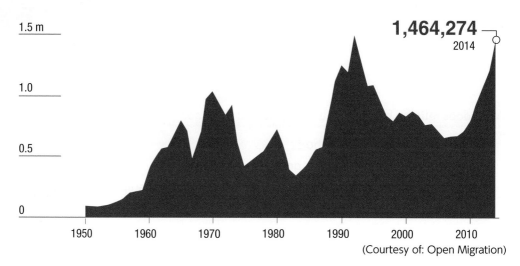

(Courtesy of: Open Migration)

This graph shows how many people immigrated to Germany. In the year of 1)_____ the number of immigrants started to increase gradually, but a few years before 1970 the number started to go 2)_____ . A couple of years after 1990 saw the biggest number of immigrants in Germany, as many as the number in 3)_____ .

Task 8 ▶ Do research and discuss

1) Germany still has many immigrants from other countries. Is this situation good for the German economy?

2) What kind of problems did Germany have when the country started to welcome many immigrants around 2014?

3) Look at the graph below. If you live in Germany, what do you think about the immigration policy in Germany?

It doesn't feel like home any more
% of people agreeing with the statement "There are so many foreigners living round here. It doesn't feel like home any more"

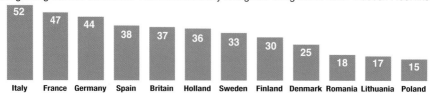

October 2016 (Source: YouGov|yougov.com)

5 Reading graphs & charts 2

Foreigners 外国人

Task 9 Fill in the blanks

02-29
069

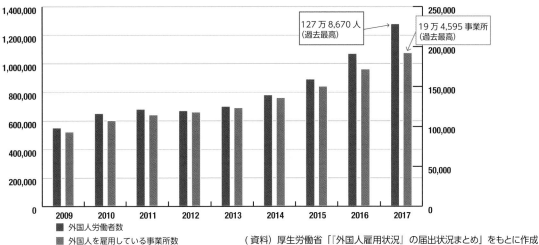

127万8,670人
（過去最高）

19万4,595事業所
（過去最高）

■ 外国人労働者数
■ 外国人を雇用している事業所数

（資料）厚生労働省「『外国人雇用状況』の届出状況まとめ」をもとに作成

This graph shows how many foreign people work in Japan. The blue bar shows the number of foreign people working in Japan, and the red bar shows the number of the working places that have foreign employees in Japan. The blue bar shows that in the year of 1)_____ the number of foreign people working in Japan was less than 600,000, but after the year the number steadily went 2)_____. The year of 3)_____ saw the biggest number of foreign people working in Japan. Also the number of the working places that have foreign employees in Japan increased year by year.

Task 10 Do research and discuss

1) Do you agree Japan has more immigrants and foreign workers?
2) What do you think about foreign people in Japan?
3) Look at the map below. From which countries do foreigners come? Why?

Foreign nationals living in Japan in 2016

■ Japan
■ 500,000+
■ 100,000 500,000
■ 10,000-50,000
■ 2,000-10,000
□ 0-2,000

(Source: Japan Statistics Bureau)

6 Discussion & presentation

CD2-30
↓ 070

Jane and Sakura are talking about cultures. What do you think about the underlined parts especially? Do you agree with their opinions?

S: Hi, Jane. Do you know that *Namahage* has been registered as a Cultural Heritage site by UNESCO?

J: Hi, Sakura. Sure. I was so surprised to hear that news.

S: Some Japanese traditions have been losing their popularity, because the number of people who practice the traditions is decreasing. I hope this registration helps Japanese traditions to be more popular in Japan as well as in other countries.

J: 1) I think Japanese people will be more interested in the culture of the countryside. When they live in an aging society, some cultural aspects are more likely to disappear.

S: What do you mean?

J: Well, recently *Namahage* folklore was in danger of losing its popularity because of the reduction of its practitioners. 2) If the youth population of Japan increases, they can expect more people to practice the tradition, but if not, the number will keep on decreasing.

S: Now, Japan should welcome more immigrants to increase its population.

J: Japan wants to increase its workforce from other countries, right?

S: That could be true. Anyway, I think we will have more chances to experience different cultures in Japan. We need to be ready for the change.

J: I agree with you, but 3) how can you prepare for it? I feel there is nothing that you can do now.

S: I disagree. There are many things that we can do. For example, we can learn about different cultures.

J: You should learn about all the different cultures.

Task 11 ▶ What do you think about immigrants and cultures? If there are more immigrants or people from other countries, you will have more cultures around you.

Engage a Lot More in Globalization

グローバル化にかかわる

1 Brainstorming

Look at the two pictures. You can see lots of spices in one picture, and a famous building in the other. Do you know what country this is? Yes, it's India. Have you visited India? What do you know about India? How do you like it?

● Warm up Talk to your classmate(s), and then listen to the explanation.

Task 1 Listen to the explanation and fill in the blanks

02-31
● 071

Vasudhaiva Kutumbakam. It is a famous saying in India which means 'the world is one
1)_____' in English. In keeping with this philosophy, India has embraced or accepted
2)_____. As India has become more globalized, there have been many positive effects,
such as a reduction in 3)_____ and an increase in life expectancy and literacy. However,
there are challenges to face as India becomes more 4)_____. For example, according to the
International Growth Centre, an organization that promotes sustainable growth in developing
countries, farmers in West Bengal were 5)_____ from their land when the government and
the large corporations wanted to use their property. It is important to find a 6)_____ of
global growth and improvement, while also respecting native lifestyle and 7)_____.

Task 2 Do shadowing

02-32
● 072

Task 3 Talk in pairs

1) Do you think India is globalized? How about Japan?
2) Which countries are globalized? Show some globalized countries. Why do you think they are globalized?
3) What does globalization mean to you?

2 Word info 1

Task 4 Match the following words with the appropriate definition.

1) globalization
   a) the interaction between people around the world
   b) the interaction and segregation of the world's people, economies, and cultures
   c) the interaction and integration of the world's people, economies, and cultures

2) multiculturalism
   a) the presence of multiple languages or cultural groups within a society
   b) the lack of multiple ethnic or cultural groups within a society
   c) the presence of multiple ethnic or cultural groups within a society

3) standard of living
   a) a level of material comfort available to a person or a group
   b) the level of psychological health of a person or a group
   c) a person's expectations of life

4) the United Nations (UN)
   a) an organization that helps maintain international peace, security, and friendly cooperative relations among nations
   b) an organization that makes the laws and regulations that all people must follow
   c) an organization that helps keep world harmony, and of which all countries in the world are a member

5) World Trade Organization (WTO)
   a) an organization where people can trade goods and services for what they want
   b) an organization that deals with the illegal trafficking of black-market items
   c) an organization that deals with the global rules of trade between nations

Task 5 Talk in pairs

1) Which word(s) mentioned above are you most interested in, and why?
2) Do you have any good ideas about how Japan is becoming more globalized?

3 Word info 2

Task 6 Fill in the blanks with the words in the box. What do you think about the global market?

> diversity   ethnicities   global market   inclusion
>
> entertainment   profitable   multiple

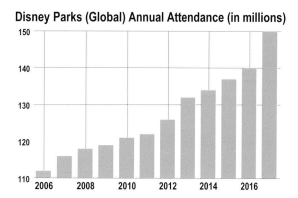

Disney Parks (Global) Annual Attendance (in millions)

Globalization can have cultural and economic effects. Cultural globalization refers to the spread of ideas or beliefs, while economic globalization refers to the 1)_____ , and the flow of free trade. For example, most people are familiar with Disney. Globalization has made it possible for people worldwide to be exposed to Disney products and ideas, and it is common for them to own 2)_____ Disney-themed items, such as stuffed animals, clothing, CDs, books, movies, or even dishware. It should not be surprising that Disney is one of the most successful media and 3)_____ businesses in the world, worth nearly 150 billion dollars. Disney theme parks can be found in Japan, France, China, and the US, and attracted approximately 150 million visitors globally in 2017. The number of annual visitors continues to increase each year. One reason that Disney has become so popular worldwide is because of its 4)_____ of characters of different 5)_____ and cultures. This focus on 6)_____ makes Disney not only powerful and 7)_____ , but also a familiar company for everyone.

4 Reading graphs & charts 1

Transport and communication costs 輸送と通信のコスト

Task 7 ▸ Fill in the blanks

CD2-33
⬇ 073

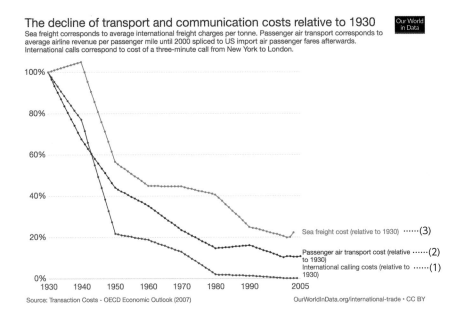

The decline of transport and communication costs relative to 1930

Sea freight corresponds to average international freight charges per tonne. Passenger air transport corresponds to average airline revenue per passenger mile until 2000 spliced to US import air passenger fares afterwards. International calls correspond to cost of a three-minute call from New York to London.

Sea freight cost (relative to 1930) ······(3)

Passenger air transport cost (relative ······(2) to 1930)

International calling costs (relative to ······(1) 1930)

Source: Transaction Costs - OECD Economic Outlook (2007)

OurWorldInData.org/international-trade • CC BY

(Source: Our World in Data: https://ourworldindata.org)

One of the factors that have contributed to rapid globalization is the decline in transport and communication 1)_____. As these costs have decreased over time, it has become 2)_____ for people to travel, and for information to spread quickly across the globe. According to the chart, (1) international calling costs, (2) passenger air transport costs, and (3) 3)_____ costs all experienced decreases from the year 1930 to 2005. In 1930, three costs were all 4)_____%. In 1950, however, (1) decreased to 21.8 %, (2) to 44.1 %, and (3) to 56.8 %. In 1980, (1) decreased to 2 %, (2) to 14.8 %, and (3) to 40.7 %. In 2003, (1) decreased to 0.1 %, (2) to 10.5 %, and (3) to 22.3 %. Transport and communication costs have considerably declined during the 5)_____ century. International calling costs especially are a sector where costs have 6)_____ significantly.

Task 8 ▸ **Do research and discuss**

1) Why have these three costs decreased?
2) Are you aware of any other costs which have decreased these days?

5 | Reading graphs & charts 2

Global exports グローバル輸出

Task 9 Fill in the blanks

02-34
074

The value of global exports
Time series of value of world exports at constant prices, relative to 1913 (i.e. values correspond to world export volumes indexed at 1913=100)

Our World in Data

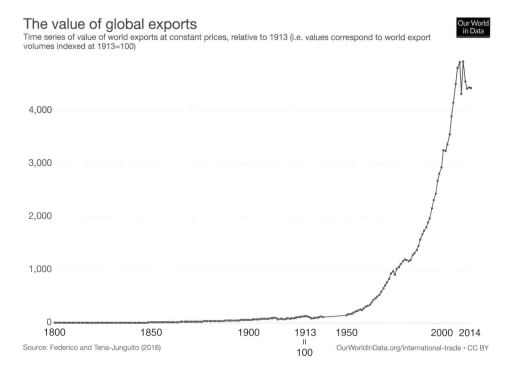

Source: Federico and Tena-Junguito (2016)   OurWorldInData.org/international-trade • CC BY

The chart above shows the value of world 1)_____ from 1800 to 2014. These estimates are in constant prices, which means they have been adjusted to account for inflation. In this chart, 1913 is set as a base year, which means the value of the index in 2)_____ is 100. This chart also shows an extraordinary 3)_____ in international trade over the last 4)_____ centuries. That is, global exports today are more than 5)_____ times larger than in 1913. The integration of national economies into a 6)_____ economic system, which is called globalization, has been greatly developed in the last century. This process of 7)_____ has led to remarkable growth in 8)_____ trade as well.

Task 10 Do research and discuss

1) Why do you think the increase happened?
2) What items in your daily life have come from overseas through international trade?

6 Discussion & presentation

Paul and Sakura are talking about multiculturalism. What do you think about the underlined parts especially? Do you agree with their opinions?

S: Wow, Paul, you use chopsticks really well.

P: Thank you. Actually, 1) <u>it is a misconception that people from non-Asian countries don't use chopsticks.</u> I've been using them since I was 6 years old.

S: Really? Did you use them when you were living in San Francisco?

P: Yes, exactly. We have many Asian restaurants there. There are many immigrants who came from Asia.

S: Yeah, I heard that the US has a lot of immigrants.

P: The US has the highest number of foreign-born residents, followed by Germany and Russia.

S: 2) <u>America must be very multicultural.</u>

P: It is. Every citizen is considered American.

S: I see. Japan is also becoming more multicultural. For example, these days many supermarkets sell Mexican tortillas. I love eating different cultural foods. I'm curious, though. Do many people have any misconceptions about Japan?

P: Before I came to Japan, I thought people ate raw fish every day.

S: That's funny. As the world becomes more globalized, we have more opportunities to learn about different cultures.

P: I agree. 3) <u>Not only within countries but also individual families, someone's culture can be unique.</u> For example, my great-grandparents are from Italy and Portugal. I love having mixed traditions and food culture in our family.

Task 11 ▸ **What do you think about multiculturalism? Do you think Japan is globalized or multicultural?**

Glossary

Unit 1

Page 13

intercultural awareness
文化間意識
▶ inter-（～間）、intercultural（文化と文化の間の、文化をまたいだ）
awareness　意識、気づき
competence　能力
UNESCO　ユネスコ（国際連合教育科学文化機関）
▶ UN- が United Nations（国際連合）を表しているので、名前が UN- で始まる機関はほとんどが国際連合のもの
synopsis　要約、大意
symbolic　象徴的な
concept　概念
sub-concept　下位概念（ある concept を組み立てる要素となっているもの）
identity　アイデンティティ、同一性
value　価値観
attitude　態度、姿勢
belief　信念、信条
dialogue (dialog)　対話
nonverbal behavior　非言語的（ことばを使わない）行動
▶ verbal　言語の
human rights　人権
clarify　明らかにする、明確にする
promote　促進する

Page 14

globalization　グローバル化
▶ globe（地球）+ -al（～の）+ -ize（～化する）+ -ation（～すること）
lifelong　一生の、生涯の
deal with ...　～を扱う、対処する
current　現在の
state　状況、状態
diversity　多様性
▶ diverse　多様な
element　（構成）要素
definition　（語句・用語などの）定義
stereotype　ステレオタイプ、偏見（「○○人は△△だ」「☆☆の人って□□だよね」などと、ある人が持つ属性によってその人の性質を決めつけてしまうこと）
multiculturalism　多文化主義（文化の多様性と異文化への寛容な姿勢を重視する考え方）
culture shock　カルチャーショック（異なる文化に出会った時に受ける衝撃）
context　文脈、状況
discomfort　不快（感）▶ comfort　快適、安楽
adjust　適応する、調節する、合わせる
unfamiliar　親しみのない、よく知らない
rely on ...　～による、たよる
interaction　交流、やり取り
▶ interact 交流する、やり取りする ▶ inter-「～間」+ act「行う、行動する」
value　価値を認める、評価する、尊重する
explicit　明白な、明示的な
▶ implicit　はっきりしない、暗示的な
apart from ...　～とは別に
fixed　固定された、決まった
racial　人種（民族）の、人種（民族）に関する
▶ race　人種、民族
regard A as B　A を B とみなす、考える
share　共有する、分かち合う、シェアする

Page 15

including ...　～を含めて
effectively　効果的に
cross-cultural　異文化間の、文化をまたいだ
interpret　理解する、解釈する
critical　批判的な、重要な
self-awareness　自己認識
second language　第二言語（たとえば、もともとポルトガル語を話すブラジル人が日本にやってきて日本語を習得し使うようになったら、その人にとってはポルトガル語が第一言語、日本語が第二言語となる）
engage in ...　～に関わる
identify with ...　～を（自己と）同一視する、自分を～と同じものと考える

Page 16

deliver　話す、（話して）伝える
media　メディア（もとは medium（通信手段、媒体）の複数形）
short-term　短期間の
▶ term　期間
explore　発見する、明らかにする
citizenship　市民性、市民意識
summarize　要約する、まとめる
▶ summary（要約、まとめ）+ -ize（～にする）
response　反応、回答
major　主な、主要な

Page 17

employee　被雇用者、（会社などの）社員
▶ employ（雇う）+ -ee（～される人）
conduct　実施する、実行する
survey　調査
according to ...　～によると
confident　自信があって
▶ be confident in ...　～に自信がある
somewhat　何らかの形で、ある程度
suggest　示す、暗示する
satisfy　満足させる
▶ be satisfied with ...　～に満足している

Page 18

prejudice　偏見、先入観
willing　前向きな、いとわない

▶ be willing to (do)　〜することをいとわない、進んで〜する

bias　偏見、先入観

Yulin　玉林（中国南部の市）

plate　皿、（一品一品の）料理

cuisine　（ある地域・文化に特徴的な）料理（の総称）

▶ Japanese cuisine　日本料理 / Chinese cuisine　中国料理

celebrate　祝う

activist　活動家

protest　抗議する

Unit 2

Page 19

fascinating　魅力的な

▶ fascinate　人を惹きつける

coexist　共存する

▶ co-（ともに）+exist（存在する）

mosque　モスク（イスラム教の寺院）

Muslim　ムスリム（イスラム教徒）

FIFA　国際サッカー連盟（Fédération Internationale de Football Association）

religious　宗教の、宗教に関する

▶ religion　宗教

side by side　（複数のものが）近くに、寄り添って

emerge　生じる、発生する

mutual　お互いの、相互の

shift　変化

▶ a shift from A to B　A から B への変化

decade　10 年間

▶ for decades　何十年もの間

Page 20

dedicate　捧げる

▶ dedicate A to B　A を B に捧げる

worship　信仰、崇拝

deity　神、天帝

synagogue　シナゴーグ（ユダヤ教の教会）

dwelling　居所、住処

describe　表現する、説明する、描写する

unconsciously　無意識のうちに

▶ un-（〜ではない）+ conscious（意識的な）+ -ly（〜に）

avoid　避ける

Page 21

appropriate　適切な

African American　アフリカ系アメリカ人（以前は black American「黒人のアメリカ人」が用いられていた）

Maori　マオリ族（の人）ニュージーランドの先住民

discrimination　差別

▶ discriminate　差別する

exclusion　排除、除外

▶ exclude　排除する、除く

indigenous　もともとある、土着の、固有の

suffer from ...　〜に苦しむ

unfair　不公平な、公正でない

▶ fair　公平な、公正な

treatment　扱い

▶ treat　扱う

immigrate　移住する（into ...）

force　強制する、無理やり〜させる

▶ force A to (do)　A に無理やり〜させる

westernize　西洋化する

▶ western（西洋の）+ -ize（〜化する）

fade　衰える、（次第に）消えていく

WWII　第二次世界大戦（World War II）

preserve　保存する、守る

bus seating　バスでの座り方

surrounding　環境

categorize　分類する

▶ category（（分けられた）種類、カテゴリー）+ -ize（〜化する）

period　時代

▶ the Edo period　江戸時代

isolate　孤立させる、隔離する

▶ be isolated from ...　〜から孤立している

governor　統治者

rule　（国などを）治める、統治する

eliminate　取り除く、除去する

underground　地下に、見えないところに

Page 22

refugee　難民

admission　受け入れ

▶ admit　入れる、受け入れる

recognition　認識、認定

▶ recognize　認識する、認定する

census　人口調査、国勢調査

gradually　徐々に、少しずつ

increase　増える、増加する

▶ decrease　減る、減少する

Ainu　アイヌ（日本の東北部〜北海道の先住民）

Page 23

concerned　気にかけて、心配して

▶ be concerned about ...　〜のことを心配する

mainstream　主流（の）

pie chart　円グラフ

upset　狼狽させる、心配させる

▶ be upset by ...　〜のせいで不安になる

ban　禁止する

reasonable　理にかなっている

economic growth　経済成長

Page 24

inconvenient　不便な

▶ convenient　便利な

affect　影響する

▶ effect　影響

negative　否定的な、よくない、マイナスの

▶ positive　肯定的な、望ましい、プラスの

wonder　疑問に思う

▶ I wonder if...　〜かどうか疑問に思う、〜なのだろうか

solve　解決する

▶ solution　解決（方法）

ethnic　民族の、民族的な

nationality　国籍（を持った人）

Unit 3

Page 25

consumer 消費者
▶ consume 消費する
voting 投票
▶ vote 投票する
ethically 倫理的に
▶ ethic 倫理 / ethical 倫理的な
palm oil パーム油（アブラヤシの実を搾って採取される植物油）
persecute 迫害する、虐げる
breed 育てる、飼育する

Page 26

mass production 大量生産
co(-)worker 職場の仲間、同僚
▶ co- （ともに）＋ worker
contribute 貢献する（to ...）
by hand 手で、手製で
diligent 勤勉な、まじめな
private school 私立学校

Page 27

eco-friendly 環境にやさしい
industrialization 産業化、工業化
▶ industry （産業、工業）＋ -al ＋ -ize ＋ -ation
fair trade フェアトレード（途上国の生産者が正当な報酬を得られるようにされた流通のしくみ）
fast fashion ファストファッション（大量生産され安価に販売される衣類）
counterpart 相当するもの、対応するもの
perspective ものの見方、考え方
demand 需要
▶ supply 供給

Page 29

traditional handicraft 伝統工芸
pop up （急に、ひょいと）上昇する
decline 減少する
machine-made 機械で作られた、機械製の
frequently 頻繁に、たびたび、しょっちゅう
similar 似ている（to ...）

Page 30

sacrifice 犠牲にする、犠牲
developing country 開発（発展）途上国
▶ developed country 先進国
give up –ing ～するのをやめる、あきらめる
purchase 買う、購入する
as well ～も、同様に
apply 適用する
appropriate 適切な

Unit 4

Page 31

believe in ... ～を信じる、信仰する
restriction 制限

▶ restrict 制限する
allow 許す、認める
▶ be allowed to (do) ～するのを許されている、～してもよい
influence 影響（on ...）
prohibit 禁じる
▶ prohibit A from ...ing A が～するのを禁じる
impure 汚れた、不潔な
protein タンパク質
instead of ... ～の代わりに
diet 食生活
exception 例外
▶ except 除く、除外する
(the) Bible 聖書

Page 32

vegetarian 菜食主義者（動物の肉を食べない人）
lacto-ovo vegetarian 乳製品と卵は食べる菜食主義者
▶ lacto- 乳の
▶ ovo ← ovum （卵、卵子）
lacto-vegetarian 乳製品は食べる菜食主義者
vegan 完全菜食主義者（動物性食品を一切摂らない人）
dairy 酪農の、乳業の（もとは「搾乳場」「バターやチーズの製造場」の意）
carbohydrates 炭水化物を多く含んだ食品
▶ carbohydrate 炭水化物
nutrition 栄養
primitive 原始的な、昔ながらの
follow （宗教を）信仰する

Page 33

eat out 外食する
obesity 肥満
utensil 用具、家庭用品
slaughterhouse 畜殺場、屠殺（とさつ）場
▶ slaughter 畜殺、屠殺
blood pressure 血圧
as a result その結果
regulation 規制、制限
▶ regulate 統制する、規制する
cruel 残酷な
▶ cruelty 残酷（さ）
process （食品を）加工する

Page 34

Veganuary ヴィーガニュアリー（完全菜食主義を広めようとする英国の慈善団体、また毎年1月に行われるその活動）
▶ vegan ＋ January （1月）
recipe 調理法、レシピ
campaign （社会的）運動、活動

Page 35

prevalence 広がり、普及
▶ prevail 広がる、流行する
rate 割合
top 頂点に達する
heart attack 心臓発作
overconsumption 摂りすぎ、過剰摂取

▶ over- (過度の) + consume (消費) + -tion (〜すること)
approach （ある目的を達成するための）方法、やり方

Page 36

disgusting　実にいやな、気持ち悪くなるような
unwell　気持ち悪い、気分がすぐれない
appetite　食欲
capture　捕まえる、とらえる
harsh　不快な、厳しい、どぎつい
absolutely　絶対に、まさしくその通り
falsely　誤って
seasoning　調味料
ingredient　原料、材料
respectful　敬意をもって、尊重して（for ...）

Unit 5

Page 37

gross　総体の、全体の
philosophy　哲学、原理
purpose　目的
based on ...　〜に基づいて
destruction　破壊
　　▶ destroy　破壊する
deforestation　森林破壊
　　▶ de-(悪化、逆転) + forest(植林する、造林する) + -ation(〜すること)
garment　衣服
measure　測る、測定する

Page 38

maternity　妊産婦の、妊産婦のための（もとは「母であること、母らしさ」の意）
　　▶ paternity　父であること、父らしさ
leave　（許可を得て取る）休暇
pregnancy　妊娠（していること）
give birth　出産する
　　▶ give birth to ...　〜を出産する
exhausted　疲れ果てた、くたくたの
　　▶ exhaust　使いつくす、へとへとに疲れさせる
except for ...　〜を除いて
pursue　追い求める、追求する
potential　可能性、潜在能力
content　満足して（with ...）
day-off / day off　休日、働かなくてよい日
benefit　利益

Page 39

burn(-)out　燃え尽き症候群（過労・ストレスによる極度の疲労）
paid holiday　有休休暇（日）
preference　好み
　　▶ prefer　〜を好む
on average　平均して
underestimate　過小評価する
　　▶ under (下に) + estimate (評価する、見積もる)
achievement　達成、成就
　　▶ achieve　達成する、成し遂げる
suicide　自殺

▶ sui (= self) + -cide (切る、殺す)
impose　課す、押し付ける

Page 40

extract　抽出する
　　▶ ex-(外に) + -tract (引く、引っ張る)

Page 41

(not) necessarily　必ずしも（〜ない）

Page 42

job hunting　求職活動（をする）、就職活動（をする）
at least　少なくとも
sustain　維持する、続ける
emit　排出する
CO_2　二酸化炭素（carbon dioxide）
atmosphere　（地球上の）大気
Maslow's Hierarchy of Needs　マズローの自己実現理論（心理学者 A・マズローが提唱した、人間の欲求を原始的欲求から自己実現に至るまで階層的に表現した理論）
material　物質、もの
in reality　現実には
sustainability　持続可能性
　　▶ sustain (持続する) + -able (〜できる) + -ity (〜さ、〜なこと)
hinder　妨げる、じゃまする

Unit 6

Page 43

as well as ...　〜と同様に
domestic　国内の
intellectual　知的な
　　▶ intellect　知性
stimulate　刺激する
　　▶ stimulus　刺激
refrain from ...　〜するのを控える、やめる

Page 44

behavior　行動、振る舞い
　　▶ behave　行動する、振る舞う
practice　行う、実行する
vernal　春の
autumnal　秋の
equinox　昼夜平分時（春分・秋分）
　　▶ equinoctial　昼夜平分時の
souvenir　土産
refer to ...　〜に言及する、〜のことを言う
ferment　発酵させる
absorb　吸収する
moisture　水分、湿気
wrap　包む
depending on ...　〜によって、〜に応じて
grind　挽く、（挽いて）粉にする

Page 45

concierge　コンシェルジェ（ホテルのロビーなどで宿泊客の希望に応じて情報提供や手配などを行う人）

overbooking　オーバーブッキング（定員以上の予約を取ること）
agent　代理人、代理店
accommodate　収容する、宿泊させる、便宜を図る
　　▶ accommodation　収容、宿泊
arrangement　手配
　　▶ arrange　手配する
transportation　交通（手段）、輸送
　　▶ transport　輸送する
B&B ＝ bed and breakfast（寝る場所と軽い朝食を提供する簡易宿泊施設）
destination　行先、目的地
temperature　温度、気温
precipitation　降水量
humidity　湿気、湿度
　　▶ humid　湿気が高い、じめじめした
duration　期間、時間（の長さ）

Page 46

inbound tourists　海外からやってくる観光客
　　▶ outbound tourists　海外へ旅行に行く観光客
annual　毎年の
in particular　特に
exponential　急激な
on the other hand　一方で

Page 47

receipt　受領高、収入
　　▶ receive　受け取る

Page 48

How did you find ...?　〜はどうでしたか、どう思いましたか
extinct　絶滅した
cassowary　ヒクイドリ
biodiversity　生物多様性
　　▶ bio-（生、生物（学）の）＋ diversity（多様性）
in danger　危険な状態の、危機に瀕している
due to ...　〜によって、〜のせいで
compound　複合物
magnificent　壮大な、見事な
fume　煙霧

Unit 7
Page 49

the Great East Japan Earthquake　東日本大震災
strike　襲う、強烈なダメージを与える
aware　気づいて、意識して
　　▶ be aware of ...　〜に気づいている、〜を意識している
community　共同体、コミュニティ
sustainable　持続可能な
encourage A to (do)　A に〜するよう促す
tolerant　寛容な
inclusive　包括した、包含した
　　▶ include　含む、包含する
dimension　側面、次元
cognitive　認知的な
socio-emotional　社会情意的な
behavioral　行動的な

domain　領域
practical　実際的な、実用的な
application　適用、応用
　　▶ apply　適用する、応用する
engagement　関わり

Page 50

belong to ...　〜に属する
local community　地域社会
residence　居住
　　▶ reside　居住する、住む
affiliation　所属、付属
　　▶ affiliate　加入させる、合併させる
duty　義務
in relation to ...　〜に関連して、関係して
migration　移住
　　▶ migrate　移住する
mobility　可動性、移動性
　　▶ mobile　可動性の、移動性のある
commitment　関わり、約束、責任
responsibly　責任をもって
　　▶ responsible　責任がある
inhabitant　住人、居住者
　　▶ inhabit　住む、居住する
societal　社会の
democracy　民主主義
North-South relations　南北関係（先進国と開発途上国との関係）
association　機構、組織、連盟

Page 51

strength　強さ、強み
　　▶ weakness　弱さ、弱み
observe　観察する
vary　変わる、変化する
empathetic　共感的な
　　▶ empathize　感情移入する、共感する
　　▶ empathy　感情移入、共感
sympathetic　同情的な
transformation　変化、変形
　　▶ transform　変化させる、変形させる
rather than ...　〜よりはむしろ

Page 52

transnational　国境を越えた、多国籍の
abide　耐える、我慢する
reconcile　和解させる、調和させる
hypernorms　ハイパー規範（人間の存在にとって基本的・原則的規範）
involve　巻き込む、関わらせる
questionnaire　アンケート（調査）
characteristic　特徴
emphasize　強調する、重視する
aspect　側面、点

Page 53

poll　世論調査
consultancy　コンサルタント業（者）

OECD　経済協力開発機構（Organization for Economic Cooperation and Development）
track　跡をたどる、追跡する
contrast　対照、対比
  ▶ by contrast　対照的に
trend　流れ、傾向

Page 54

nationalism　国家主義
background　背景、背後にある事情

Unit 8

Page 55

education　教育
  ▶ educate　教育する
figure　図、図表
chart　図、図表
tuition　授業料
revenue　収入
  ▶ expenditure　支出
teaching material　教材
source　源
primary　初期の、一次的な
  ▶ primary education　初等教育
secondary　二次的な
  ▶ secondary education　中等教育
majority　大部分、多数（派）
  ▶ minority　少数（派）
work part time　非常勤で働く、アルバイトをする
  ▶ work full time　常勤で（正規社員として）働く

Page 56

tertiary　三次的な
  ▶ tertiary education　高等教育
elementary　初等の、初期の
graduate school　大学院
bachelor　学士
master　修士
doctor　博士
degree　学位
correspondence　通信
institute　（教育）機関、専門学校、大学（校）

Page 57

official　公式の
informal　非公式の、略式の
private　私的な、私立の
budget　予算
expense　費用
dropout　中途退学
surgical operation　外科手術
quit　やめる
enrollment　入学、就学
  ▶ enrollment rate　就学率
index　指標
burden　負荷、重荷
attend　出席する

graduation ceremony　卒業式、修了式

Page 58

glance　一見、一目
  ▶ at a glance　一見して、一目見て
investigate　調べる、調査する
whereas　一方で、その一方
distribution　分配、配分
  ▶ distribute「配る、配分する、分配する」
in terms of ...　〜の点で

Page 60

sociology　社会学
semester　学期
credit　（授業科目の）単位
matter　重要である
  ▶ It doesn't matter...　〜はたいしたことではない、あまり関係ない
transfer　移す、動かす
flexible　柔軟な
sound　〜に聞こえる、〜に思われる
be planning to (do)　〜しようと考えている
be worth ...ing　〜する価値がある

Unit 9

Page 61

literature　文学
visual　視覚的な
graphic　図示的な
plastic　造形の
decorative　装飾の
perform　行う、演じる
architecture　建築（物）
creativity　創造性
  ▶ create　創る、創造する
imagination　想像力
  ▶ imagine　想像する、思い浮かべる
express　表現する
in addition　加えて、さらに
emotion　感情
inspire　刺激する、（刺激して）〜させる

Page 62

convey　運ぶ、伝える
aesthetic　美的な、美に関する
valuable　価値がある
abstract　抽象的な
concrete　具体的な
realistic　現実的な、実際的な
depiction　描写、叙述
  ▶ depict　描写する、描く
artisan　職人
renaissance　ルネサンス（文芸復興）
revival　復活、復興
  ▶ revive　復活する、復興する

Page 63

donation　寄付
fund　基金（を集める）
gallery　画廊、美術館
accessible　接することができる
　　▶ access　近寄る、接近する
regardless of ...　～に関わらず
run short　不足する
BBC　英国放送協会（British Broadcasting Cooperation）
facility　施設、設備
maintain　維持する
financial　経済的な、予算上の
bar graph　棒グラフ
inflation　（通貨）膨張、インフレーション
invest　投資する
per ...　～1つ（1人）につき
reduction　低下、減少
　　▶ reduce　減らす、少なくする

Page 64

correlation　相関（関係）
　　▶ co-（ともに）+ relation（関係、関わり）
throughout　～にわたって、～全体で
satisfaction　満足
　　▶ satisfy　満足させる
accurately　正確に

Page 65

export　輸出（する）
　　▶ import　輸入（する）
Eurostat　ユーロスタット（欧州委員会統計局）
meanwhile　一方で
audio-visual　音響と映像の
rural　郊外の、田舎の
expect　予期する、予想する

Page 66

contemporary　現代の
temporary　一時的な、仮の
exhibition　展示（会）
　　▶ exhibit　展示する
inventor　発明者
cubism　立体派、キュービズム
genius　天才
polymath　博学者
talented　才能がある
　　▶ talent　才能（のある人）
provide　提供する

Unit 10

Page 67

artificial intelligence (AI)　人工知能
vehicle　乗り物
desert　砂漠、沙漠
expert　専門家
illusion　幻覚、錯覚
humanity　人間性

MIT　マサチューセッツ工科大学（Massachusetts Institute of Technology）
roboticist　ロボット工学の専門家
　　▶ robotics　ロボット工学
collaboration　協働、コラボレーション
　　co-（ともに）+ labor（働く）+ -ation（～すること）
acquire　獲得する、修得する

Page 68

devote　捧げる
appliance　機器、器具、設備
device　装置
detect　感知する
physical property　物理的性質

Page 69

code　記号、暗号、（プログラムの）コード
customize　状況に応じて作る（作り変える）
virtual　仮想の、虚像の
DNA　デオキシリボ核酸（deoxyribonucleic acid）
partnership　共同、協力関係
document　書類
viewable　見える、視認できる
fix　直す、修正する
error　誤り、（プログラム上の）エラー
existence　存在
　　▶ exist　存在する
technology giant　テクノロジーの巨人（ICT業界の最大手会社）

Page 70

page views　ページの閲覧
spike　急上昇する
web traffic　ウェブ上の通信（量）
organic　本質的な、本物の
marketing　市場取引（売買）
instead　その代わりに、そうではなく
rapid　速い、急速な

Page 71

natural science　自然科学
engineering and technology　工学
agricultural science　農学
social science　社会科学
humanities　人文学
harvest　収穫する
focus　焦点
compile　集める、編集する、まとめる
sector　分派、グループ
industry　産業
　　▶ food industry　食品産業

Page 72

laboratory　研究所、研究室
conference　会議、大会、学会
manufacture　製造する
unemployed　仕事がない、職についていない
judgment　判断
security　安全、治安

consider　考える、熟慮する
ease　簡単さ、容易さ
　▶ with ease　簡単に、容易に
assistance　補助、援助
　▶ assist　援助する、補助する

Unit 11

Page 73

gender　性、性別、ジェンダー（社会的・文化的な意味における性、生物的な「性、性別」は sex）
be set to (do)　〜する用意ができている、〜することになっている
absolute monarchy　絶対君主制（の国）
conservative　保守的な
　▶ radical / progressive　革新的な
Wahhabism　ワッハーブ派（イスラム教の保守的な宗派）
guardian　保護者、守護者
crown prince　皇太子
decree　法令、制令
modernization　近代化
　▶ modern（近代的な）+ -ize（〜化する）+ -ation（〜すること）
driver's license　運転免許
removal　除去、廃止
　▶ remove　取り除く
divorce　離婚する
　▶ marry　結婚する

Page 74

practice　（柔道・相撲などを）する、やる（play judo とはあまり言わない）
previous　前の、以前の

Page 75

household chores　（いろいろな）家事
regularly　規則的に、いつものように
national assembly　国の議会、国会
representative　代表者、代議士、議員
multitasking　マルチタスキング（複数の仕事を同時に行うこと）
position　（ある組織の中での）立場、役職
cram school　塾、予備校

Page 76

generally speaking　一般的に、概して言えば
take over　（仕事などを）引き受ける

Page 77

tendency　傾向
　▶ tend (to do)　〜する傾向がある

Page 78

complaint　不平、不満
　▶ complain　不平を言う、不満を言う
fixed　決まった、固定的な
run for ...　〜に出馬する、立候補する

Unit 12

Page 79

cashless　現金を使わない
　▶ cash（現金）+ -less（〜がない）
wallet　財布、札入れ
　▶ purse　財布、小銭入れ
prepaid　前払いの、先に入金して使う
　▶ pre-（前の）+ paid「（支払われた）」
recharge　再び入金する、再チャージする
　▶ re-（再び）+ charge（入金する）
thanks to ...　〜のおかげで、〜によって

Page 80

virtual currency　仮想通貨
monetary unit　通貨単位
ownership　所有（していること）
per capita　（国民）1人につき
　▶ per ...　〜につき
reluctant　躊躇して、嫌がって
cryptocurrency　暗号通貨、仮想通貨
aging society　高齢化社会

Page 81

leak　（液体・気体・光・情報などが）漏れる
　▶ leakage　漏れること、漏えい
advanced　進んだ、進化した
application　アプリケーション、アプリ（英語では appli ではなく app と略す）
store　保管する、取っておく
trace　跡をたどる、追跡する
digitize　デジタル化する
precisely　正確に、精密に
enhance　高める、強化する
earning　儲け、稼ぎ
　▶ earn　稼ぐ、儲ける
overproduction　過剰生産
　▶ over-（過度の）+ produce（生産する）+ -tion（〜すること）
hacker　ハッカー（コンピュータシステムに侵入し情報を盗んだり操作したりする人）
　▶ hack（斧などの刃物で乱暴に）たたき切る、ぶった切る
fame　名声、有名であること
　▶ famous　有名な
compensate　償う、補う

Page 82

contrary to ...　〜とは反対に、〜に反して
latter　（順番が）後の方の、（2つのうちの）2つめの、後半の（late の比較級）

Page 83

double　倍になる
　▶ triple　3倍になる
in that sense　その意味では、その点では
reliable　信頼できる、頼れる
　▶ rely（頼る）+ -able（〜できる）

Page 84

confuse　混乱させる
pros and cons　賛成（意見）と反対（意見）、賛否
PIN　personal identification number（個人識別番号、暗証番号）
debit　（帳簿の）借り方
▶ debit card　預金口座から直接代金を引くカード
distinguish　区別する

Unit 13

Page 85

pray　祈る
▶ prayer　祈り
in common　共通して
quote　引用（した言葉・文章）
violent　暴力的な
▶ violence　暴力
ironically　皮肉にも
▶ irony　皮肉
neutral　中立の
military draft　徴兵

Page 86

alliance　同盟
▶ ally　同盟を結ぶ
interfere　干渉する、口出しをする
infect　感染させる
virus　病原菌、ウイルス
anonymous　匿名の、名前がわからない
browse　拾い読みする、（インターネットで）情報を検索する
flash drive　（持ち運びできる小型の）データ保存用メモリ
cyber　コンピュータの、ネットワーク上の

Page 87

nuclear warhead　核弾頭
firearm　火器、小火器（ピストルなど）
self-defense　自己防衛、自衛
renewable　再生可能な
▶ re-（再び）+ new（新しい）+ -able（できる）
suspicious　疑わしい、あやしい、不審な
smack　たたく、平手打ちする
generate　引き起こす、発生させる

Page 88

legally　合法的に

Page 89

arsenal　兵器庫、兵器工場
explosion　爆発
▶ explode　爆発する

Page 90

mutually　相互に、互いに
to be honest　正直に言うと、正直なところ
negative peace　消極的平和（直接的な暴力・戦争がない状態）
▶ positive peace　積極的平和（争いの原因となる構造的な暴力がない状態）

Unit 14

Page 91

wrestle　取っ組み合う、苦闘する
climax　絶頂、最高潮

Page 92

permanent　永久の、永続的な
▶ permanent residence　永住
civil war　内戦

Page 93

a bunch of ...　たくさんの〜（= a lot of ...）
▶ bunch　（果物の）房、（花などの）束
alien　外国人、異星人
amusement park　遊園地

Page 94

a couple of ...　数〜、いくつかの〜
▶ a couple of years after 1990　1990 年から数年たって

Page 95

steadily　着実に、確実に
▶ steady　しっかりした、安定した

Page 96

register　登録する
▶ registration　「登録」
disappear　消える、消滅する
▶ dis-（否定）+ appear（現れる、出現する）
folklore　民間伝承、民俗
practitioner　実践者
workforce　労働力

Unit 15

Page 97

embrace　抱擁する、包含する、受け入れる
life expectancy　平均余命、寿命
literacy　読み書きの能力、識字能力
face　直面する
the International Growth Centre　ロンドン・スクール・オブ・エコノミクスに付属する開発途上国支援組織
corporation　法人、企業

Page 98

segregation　分離、隔離
integration　融合、統合
lack　欠乏、欠けていること
material　物質的な
psychological　心理的な
▶ psychology　心理学
cooperative　協力的な
▶ cooperate　協力する（co-「ともに」+ operate「働く、仕事をする」）
harmony　調和
goods　商品

illegal trafficking　違法売買

Page 99

ethnicity　民族性
multiple　多様な、多くの部分からなる
expose　さらす、触れさせる
　▶ be exposed to ...　〜に接する、さらされる
stuffed animal　動物のぬいぐるみ

Page 100

considerably　かなり、相当に
significantly　はっきりと、顕著に

Page 101

adjust　調整する、調節する
extraordinary　異常な、並外れた
　▶ extra-（〜を超えた）+ ordinary（通常の）
remarkable　顕著な、はっきりした

Page 102

misconception　思い違い、誤解
tortilla　トルティーヤ（トウモロコシ粉で作った薄いパンケーキ）
curious　好奇心のある、知りたがりの
..., though　（文末に用いて）〜なのだが、〜なんだけどね
unique　独特な、唯一の

著者

笹島　茂 (ささじま　しげる)

工藤泰三 (くどう　たいぞう)

荊　紅涛 (けい　こうとう)

Larry Joe (ラリー　ジョー)

Hannah Haruna (ハナ　ハルナ)

クリル えいご つちか ぶんかかんいしき
CLIL 英語で培う文化間意識

2020 年 2 月 20 日　第 1 版発行
2024 年 3 月 10 日　第 7 版発行

著　者　　笹島　茂
　　　　　　工藤泰三
　　　　　　荊　紅涛
　　　　　　Larry Joe
　　　　　　Hannah Haruna

発行者　前田俊秀
発行所　株式会社　三修社
　　　　　〒 150-0001 東京都渋谷区神宮前 2-2-22
　　　　　TEL　　03-3405-4511
　　　　　FAX　　03-3405-4522
　　　　　振替　　00190-9-72758
　　　　　https://www.sanshusha.co.jp
　　　　　編集担当　永尾真理

DTP　藤原志麻
表紙デザイン　岩泉卓屋
印刷　壮光舎印刷株式会社

© 2020 Printed in Japan ISBN978-4-384- 33494-4 C1082